SALTWATER KITCHEN COOKBOOK

CORNISH FOOD ADVENTURES FROM THE BEACH TO THE TABLE

BY LOUISE SEARLE AND HAYLEY SPURWAY

SALTWATER KITCHEN COOKBOOK

CORNISH FOOD ADVENTURES FROM THE BEACH TO THE TABLE

BY LOUISE SEARLE AND HAYLEY SPURWAY

Editor: Louise Searle
Writer: Hayley Spurway
Photographer: Mike Searle
Designer: David Alcock
Proof reader: Alex Hapgood

Photographic contributors: Kirstin Prisk, Kate Czuczman/Neon, Emily Furness, Louise Searle, Carla Regler, Jonny Noakes, Steve England, Zack Searle, Greg Martin • All photos ©Mike Searle except on pages 134, 153, ©Carla Regler; 57, 62 , 80, 94, 103, 134, 189 ©Louise Searle; 80, 142 ©Steve England; 12, 17 ©Jonny Noakes; 56 ©Kate Czuczman/Neon; 150 ©Greg Martin; 136, 154 ©Zack Searle; 78, 83 ©Kirstin Prisk; 114, 115 ©Emily Furness; 94 ©Shutterstock/PopTika; 91, 111, 142, 169, 110 ©Shutterstock; 52 ©Chris Cypert courtesy Scarlet Hotel
Cover: Alfie England

Saltwater Cookbook ISBN 978-0-9932336-0-9
www.saltwaterkitchen.com

Printed and bound: Four Way Print Ltd, Cornwall
Published by Muse Media, www.musemedia.co.uk
Publisher: Steve England

TAKE A
BITE OF
BEACH LIFE

It's no secret that Cornwall has become something of a gastronomic hotspot. Lip-smacking ingredients grown, reared and plucked from its coastal beauty are being flipped onto plates to great applaud. At a time when people are starting to wake up to the provenance of their food, it's little wonder that Cornwall is in the spotlight: here you only have to look out to sea, stroll along the cliffs and tramp across rolling pastures to see where your food has come from.

In the Saltwater Kitchen Cookbook we've unearthed a collection of people who are passionate about food. Their mission is to create delicious, homemade food inspired by the sea and their surroundings. We've got under the skin of Cornwall's foodie revolution and collected recipes, tips and inspiration from these culinary artisans whose lifestyles, ingredients and cooking are engrained in the coastal lifestyle.

Learn how to take the Saltwater Kitchen approach to your cooking and bring the coastal life to your table: create gourmet feasts from foraged ingredients, sizzle up seasonal lunches for carefree summer days and find out where to source seafood flipped straight from the day boats. Or you can simply slink off and dine on down-to-earth cuisine in Cornwall's finest surfside restaurants.

TUCK IN AND TASTE THIS COASTAL CUISINE

CONTENTS

THE ATLANTIC HIGHWAY

BIKES AND BOARDS, SALTY BREEZE IN YOUR HAIR, HEARTY FOODS ALL STYLED WITH EASE

BURGERS, BURRITOS, BIKES AND BEACH HUTS

Step foot on the wild surf beaches, untrammelled coast path and wave-hewn headlands of Cornwall's unspoilt North Coast. A land of eye-popping scenery, the Atlantic lashes at its shores and moulds the character of villages wedged between waves and rolling countryside. Linking the coastline from Newquay to Bude and beyond is Cornwall's Atlantic Highway – an artery for surfers, motorcyclists and visitors freewheeling between the beaches and plunging into coastal activities at every pit stop.

Strung around Trevose Head, within easy reach of St Merryn, is a necklace of seven bays: go snorkelling at Porthcothan, leap into the tidal pool at Treyarnon, ride the waves at Constantine and Booby's, build sandcastles on Mother Ivey's, paddleboard at Harlyn and swim at Trevone. Between Polzeath and Bude the beaches peter out – a smattering of wild coves dominated by craggy cliffs and calf-busting sections of coast path boasting staggering views.

A BUSY BEACH LIFE SUMMONS UP GARGANTUAN APPETITES, MET BY A BURGEONING FOOD AND DRINK SCENE. While Padstow may have pioneered North Cornwall's foodie revolution, lesser-known villages and talented local chefs are hitting the gourmet bull's-eye with laid-back coastal cooking drawing on the abundance of sumptuous local produce.

BURGERS & BIKES

{STRONG ADOLFO'S}

On the Atlantic Highway, within easy reach of St Merryn's seven bays and bang-on the main artery between North Cornwall's surf breaks, John and Mathilda Friström Eldridge have opened Strong Adolfo's. A trendy roadside café inspired by the coastal lifestyle on the doorstep, here great food is served alongside lashings of surf and motorcycle culture.

"We're both really into motorbikes and surfing. This is a really great road to ride on your motorbike, and also links some of the best surf breaks on the North Cornwall coast," explains John. "We get a lot of surfers coming here – they might have surfed somewhere up the coast, and stop in for lunch on the way to another surf spot somewhere down the coast." Despite not being beachside, the location has been a hit: surfers storm the place for pre-surf smoothies, post dawnie breakfasts, or warming bowls of Masoor Dal. Bikers congregate here for burgers and coffee on regular bike nights. Families and creative types flock here too.

"I THINK PEOPLE LIKE US BECAUSE WE'RE SOMETHING DIFFERENT IN CORNWALL. We've taken influences from all over the world and created a café individual to our personalities," says Mathilda.

While the stripped-back industrial interior with movie-poster artwork and a lick of vintage style is indicative of the couple's unique style, it's the food that truly expresses their lifestyle and passions. Alongside big breakfasts – using locally produced sausages and bacon, home-made baked beans, and slow-roasted tomatoes and mushrooms – there is also a healthy granola with cardamom, inspired by the couple's favourite café in Bali where they met while travelling. The broader menu is a mix of classic café food with more adventurous specials inspired by dishes from all around the world. The pulled pork burger is one of the most popular items, with smoked paprika onion rings, chips, homemade coleslaw and head-chef Katie Gillmon's unbelievable BBQ sauce.

Adding a sprinkling of foodie culture from Mathilda's homeland of Sweden, Swedish Fika – sweet treats served with coffee – is a big influence behind the impressive display of homemade cakes and cookies. "Not all of my cakes are Swedish in their style, it's more about the culture of having coffee with a sweet treat," she explains. "There might be Swedish chocolate balls and cinnamon buns alongside more traditional English sponge cakes. I try and do lots of gluten-free cooking too, such as gluten-free Swedish mud cakes and chocolate brownies."

Driven by their passion for food, travel and the coast, Mathilda and John's enterprise goes hand-in-hand with their lifestyle. Like many of their customers, when they're not in the café, they're out catching waves or cruising the coast road on their motorbikes. "It's always a good reason to get up in the morning – to get on your motorbike and check the surf," says Mathilda. "Our favourite ride is the Atlantic Highway all the way to Bude and on to Devon, or even south past Newquay and onto West Cornwall and Sennen."

Strong Adolfo's Slow Roast Pulled Pork Shoulder

Serves 6

Ingredients

- Large boned and unrolled pork shoulder (your butcher will do this for you)
- 3 white onions
- 1 orange
- 1 leek
- 2 large carrots
- 1 bulb of garlic
- Bunch of thyme
- Bunch of rosemary
- 1 bottle (500ml) cider (we use Cornish Orchards Heritage)

Method

1. Quarter the onions, orange, leek and carrots and lay them in a large, deep baking tray. Scatter the cloves of garlic and herbs over the vegetables. The vegetables are acting as a trivet to protect the pork while also adding flavour and moisture.
2. Pour over cider and if needed top up with cold water to roughly 2 inches from the top of the tray (the pork will create its own juices as it cooks).
3. Season the underside of the pork with salt and pepper.
4. Lay the pork onto the vegetable trivet skin side up. Season the skin with salt and rub with olive oil, there's no need to score it.
5. Cover with foil and cook in middle shelf of the oven for 7-8 hours at 140C (fan).
6. When cooked, carefully uncover the pork. Pull at the meat, if it easily pulls away it is ready.
7. The skin can be lifted away from the meat and if required can be cooked on another baking tray at 200C for 10 minutes to get good crackling.
8. Lift meat from its vegetable trivet and pull it apart. Serve with the Oriental BBQ sauce for Strong Adolfo's take on Pulled Pork.

Oriental Style BBQ Sauce

Ingredients

- 1 onion
- 4 garlic cloves
- 500ml (18fl oz) Hoisin sauce
- 500ml (18fl oz) tomato ketchup
- 200ml (7fl oz) brown sauce
- 500ml (18fl oz) orange juice
- 2 star anise
- 2 cinnamon sticks
- 150g (5½oz) dark brown sugar

Method

1. Roughly chop the onion and heat a little olive oil in a large pan over a medium heat.
2. Lightly fry the onions to soften, then add roughly chopped garlic and gently fry.
3. Next add 2 star anise and 2 cinnamon sticks.
4. Now add the rest of the ingredients.
5. Bring to a gentle simmer and take off the heat and allow to cool a little before passing through a sieve.

To serve place pulled pork in a toasted bap or brioche and smother with BBQ sauce... delish!

Masoor Dal

Masoor Dal was the first truly vegan dish to appear on our specials board and since its introduction a variation of this dish has appeared on the menu everyday due to popular demand. This Dal is simple to prepare, flavoursome and healthy. You'll even find hearty meat eaters will devour this dish in a wolf-like fashion.

Ingredients
- 1 onion
- 5 garlic cloves
- 500g (17½oz) dried red lentils
- 2 tins of coconut milk
- 1 tsp chilli powder
- 2 tsp curry powder
- 1 ½ tbsp garam masala
- 1 tbsp turmeric
- ½ tbsp cumin seeds
- 2 limes, zest and juice
- ½ ltr (17½fl oz) of vegetable stock (add more stock if it dries out when cooking)

Method
1. In a large pan heat some vegetable oil over a medium heat. Finely dice the onion, add to pan and gently fry for a few minutes. Crush and chop the garlic and add to the onions.
2. After a few minutes of frying add the spices and gently fry – taking care not to let the spices burn.
3. Next add the lentils (no need to wash), followed by the coconut milk, lime juice and stock.
4. Leave to simmer on a low to medium heat for about half an hour, regularly stirring to ensure it doesn't stick.
5. Cook until lentils are tender, then season with salt. (Season after the lentils are cooked as salt at the beginning will prevent them from softening.)
6. Serve with pitta.

Coriander Chutney

We think coriander chutney is a fresh and uplifting topping for our Masoor Dal.

- 100g (3½oz) fresh coriander, stalks and all
- 2 thumb-size pieces of ginger
- 1 lime, juice of
- ½ large onion
- 2 tbsp dark muscovado sugar
- 1 red chilli, finely chopped
- 2 tbsp desiccated coconut

Blitz onion and ginger in a food processor until fine. Then add the rest of the ingredients and pulse until it becomes a dry paste.

WHAT'S FIKA?

Fika is big part of the Swedish coffee culture. It basically means a coffee break with a sweet treat. According to Mathilda, it is usual for Swedes to take Fika at least three times a day. "There's always a moment for Fika in Sweden. People will even go out in the evening for coffee and cake. It's grounded in their social lives," she says.

The tradition is thought to derive from Kafferep – a kind of Scandinavian high tea harking back to the 1900s. It was usual for seven different types of cakes or cookies to be served as part of these tea parties, which were usually part of a social meeting for ladies to show off their baking skills. The popularity of kafferep waned, but has since seen a revival in stylish restaurants and cafés across Scandinavia.

Cinnamon buns, chocolate balls and cookies are typical treats served for Fika, but Mathilda explains that the cakes she makes don't have to be traditionally Swedish, and she gleans inspiration from all sorts of recipe books and cookery blogs. "I bake from the heart," she explains. "It's the Scandinavian way to have quality, not quantity."

Mathilda's Raspberry and Meringue Cake

This cake is such a lovely combination of different layers, textures and flavours. Vanilla and almond sponge cake meets the sharp freshness of the raspberries, topped with sweet meringue that is crunchy on the top yet soft in the middle. Use any fruit or berries depending on the season, although we'd recommend them to be on the tart side to balance the sweetness of the meringue.

Ingredients

Cake mix:
- 225g (8oz) butter
- 140g (5oz) sugar
- 2 eggs
- 1 egg yolk (keep the egg white in a clean, dry small bowl and make sure no yolk goes in with the white)
- ½ tsp almond oil
- 1 tsp vanilla bean paste
- 220g (7½oz) flour
- 1½ tsp baking powder
- 200g (7oz) raspberries

Meringue:
- 3 egg whites – weigh these then double the amount to work out how much sugar to use
- Sugar – twice the weight of the egg whites
- 40g (1½oz) ground almonds
- 1-2 handfuls flaked almonds to decorate

Method

Pre-heat the oven to 150C (fan)

Cake:
1. Melt the butter. Whisk the eggs, egg yolk and sugar until light and airy.
2. Add the almond oil, vanilla bean paste and melted butter to the egg mixture.
3. Sieve in the flour and baking powder. Fold together until combined.

Meringue:
1. Make sure all bowls and whisks are clean and dry – keep any yolk out of the egg whites, use metal bowls and spoons, no plastic.
2. Whisk the egg whites until stiff peaks are formed. Add the sugar little by little and let it whisk well. Add a small squeeze of lemon. Keep whisking until the meringue is thick and glossy and all sugar is dissolved. Fold in the ground almonds using a metal spoon.

Assembly:
1. Lightly grease a 24cm round baking tin and line with baking parchment.
2. Pour in the cake mix and top with the raspberries. Spoon the meringue on top and leave a gap between the meringue and the side of the baking tin.
3. Top the meringue with a handful or two of flaked almonds and sprinkle some down the sides around the meringue to fill the gap (this prevents the meringue sticking to the sides and rising unevenly)
4. Bake on 150C in the middle of the oven for 55-60 minutes. Insert a skewer to check that the middle of the cake is baked (a few crumbs on the skewer is fine but it shouldn't look wet). The cake might not seem set, but will do so when left to cool completely.

Chocolate Mud Cake (Gluten Free)

This is a rich and gooey chocolate cake for all chocolate lovers. If you don't have enough time to make the ganache, just dust with icing sugar and serve while warm with vanilla ice cream or Chantilly cream. Mud cake or 'Kladdkaka' is very popular in Sweden; here we've created our own version of it.

Ingredients

- 320g (11oz) butter
- 4 eggs
- 340g (12oz) sugar
- 140g (5oz) muscovado sugar
- 1 tsp vanilla bean paste
- 170g (6oz) gluten free flour (we use Doves)
- 80g (3oz) good quality cocoa powder
- 2 tsp baking powder (make sure it's gluten free)

Method

1. Preheat the oven to 150C (fan)
2. Start by melting the butter.
3. Whisk the eggs and sugar in a mixing bowl briefly until combined. Add the vanilla bean paste and the melted butter to the egg mixture then sieve in the flour, cocoa powder and baking powder. Fold together until combined.
4. Grease a 24cm diameter round baking tin and cut a circle of baking parchment to cover the bottom of the tin. Either dust the sides of the tin with cocoa powder or cover with strips of baking parchment.
5. Pour in the mixture and even out the top. Bake in the middle of the oven for about 45-50 minutes. Insert a skewer to check the consistency – it should be quite gooey in the middle.
6. Leave to cool completely if you're covering the cake with ganache, or eat it while still warm and serve with vanilla ice cream.

Dark Chocolate Ganache

Ingredients

- 200g (7oz) good quality dark chocolate (we use Green & Blacks 70%)
- 280ml double cream

Method

1. Finely chop the chocolate and place in a bowl.
2. Heat the double cream in a saucepan until 80C (almost boiling) then set aside for a few minutes. Pour the cream into a jug (to bring down the temperature) and wait until the cream is just above 50C.
3. Pour the cream over the chocolate and stir together to a smooth ganache. Leave to cool until desired consistency.
4. Place the cake on a cooling rack then start to cover the top with ganache. Use a large palette knife or spatula and circle it around the top, start in the middle and work your way towards the edges until it drips down the sides. Cover the top with your favourite berries then leave to cool in the fridge for a few minutes until the ganache is set.

DITCH YOUR SURFBOARDS AT THE DOOR!

{SURF STYLE EATERIES}

Here are our top five bang-on-the-beach cafés inspired by the surf lifestyle:

■ LIFE'S A BEACH, BUDE

By day Life's A Beach poses as a simple seaside café where surfers almost ride past the windows at high tide. But by night it scrubs up into a top-notch seafood bistro, serving the freshest catch flipped straight from Bude's fishing boats into the frying pan. The most famous dish is the salt-baked bream, but it's not all seafood on the menu - there's local meats and game to be enjoyed too. www.lifesabeach.info

■ THE BEACH HUT, WATERGATE BAY

Shake off the saltwater and hang out in one of Newquay's coolest beachside cafés. Don't let surfboards, sandy feet and dogs lolling under the tables fool you into thinking this place is so laid back about its approach to food: the classic bistro cuisine is some of the best you'll find served by any beach in Cornwall. From lazy brunches to gourmet dinners, the dishes are stuffed with local ingredients and cooked to perfection. www.watergatebay.co.uk/food-and-drink/the-beach-hut

■ THE STRAND CAFÉ, TREBARWITH STRAND

Sitting beside the Atlantic-lashed caves, cliffs and sugary sands of Trebarwith Strand is The Strand Café, serving wholesome food from crab sandwiches to Cornish cream teas. Tuck into homemade nut-burgers, delectable cakes and seasonal salads with a gob-smacking backdrop, or take away your feast to enjoy on the beach. www.thestrandcafe.co.uk

■ PORTHMEOR BEACH CAFÉ, ST IVES

Tapas using the finest, freshest produce is at the heart of this retro-cool café overhanging St Ives' most famous surf beach. Chill out surfside for a cracking breakfast, or sink a sundowner and graze your way through the tapas menu from salt and pepper squid to harissa-grilled mackerel. There's even blankets to snuggle up under if you insist on alfresco dining on cooler evenings. www.porthmeor-beach.co.uk/cafe

■ GODREVY BEACH CAFÉ, GODREVY

It's not just consistent waves, the iconic lighthouse and miles of sand that beckon crowds to Godrevy. Tucked behind the dunes, the Godrevy Beach Café attracts flocks of sandy-soled punters to feast on home-baked cakes, hearty breakfasts, doorstep sandwiches and lunch platters stuffed with fresh Cornish ingredients. Made for all weathers - you can hunker down on the sofa or bask on the decking. www.godrevycafe.co.uk

BREEZE IN YOUR HAIR, SALT ON YOUR SKIN

Neil Haydock spent his childhood shooting pheasants and rabbits with his Grandfather, and living off 'proper' food plucked from the Lancashire countryside. Having worked his way through high profile restaurants in London and the Caribbean, he was lured to the West Country to help set up Fifteen Cornwall. Now, as the Executive Chef across Watergate Bay Hotel's restaurants, he's at the helm of the bay's original eatery: The Beach Hut.

Pairing his passion for American cuisine with The Beach Hut's laid-back style, Neil has launched a new Sunday brunch surfside.

"BRUNCH GOES HAND-IN-HAND WITH THE BEACH HUT ETHOS; WHEN YOU'RE EATING BRUNCH YOU JUST KNOW YOU'RE ON HOLIDAY," he says. Creating a versatile dining experience to suit different moods and tastes, you can get a full fry up or poached eggs, alongside a signature burger or a steaming pot of St Austell Bay mussels. "It's not unusual for one diner to have pancakes, while another on the same table is devouring a roast chicken," says Neil.

Haydock's favourite brunch dish is Eggs Benedict – served at The Beach Hut with huge Cornish field mushrooms. "It's the sort of dish you can tweak with your favourite ingredients – such as Spanish chorizo or Italian prosciutto – to give it a holiday feel. Once in the US Keys I had a version served with lobster and key lime hollandaise," says Neil.

Eggs Portobello

There are many variances of Eggs Benedict, from avocado and smoked salmon to black pudding. Here's The Beach Hut's version, with Portobello mushrooms – perfect for Sunday brunch.

Serves 4

Ingredients
- 2 crushed black peppercorns
- Bay leaf
- 200ml (7fl oz) white wine vinegar
- 250g (9oz) clarified butter
- 4 egg yolks
- Cornish sea salt
- 1 lemon
- Paprika
- Ground black pepper
- 8 field or Portobello mushrooms, cleaned and stalk removed
- 1 sprig of thyme
- 100g (3½oz) unsalted butter
- 8 fresh, free-range eggs
- 4 thick slices of your favourite bread

Method

1. Put the peppercorns, bay leaf and vinegar in a pan, bring to the boil and reduce by half.
2. Heat the clarified butter in a separate pan, until fully melted, and take off the heat.
3. Pass the vinegar reduction through a sieve into a bowl, removing the peppercorns and bay leaf - insert vinegar.
4. Add the 4 egg yolks and place the bowl over a simmering pan of water and whisk until light and airy.
5. Gradually add the clarified butter to the eggs, whisking continuously until all the butter is incorporated. Season with salt, lemon and paprika, and keep warm.
6. Put the mushrooms onto a tray and season with salt and pepper.
7. Strip the thyme leaves and sprinkle over the mushrooms. Add a knob of butter and place under the grill until cooked, then keep warm.
8. Place a large pan of water on to boil, add a little salt and a splash of white wine vinegar.
9. Once boiling, crack the eggs into the water to poach. When cooked, but still soft in the middle, remove and keep warm.
10. Toast the bread and lightly butter. Top with two mushrooms per slice and place a poached egg on each mushroom. Spoon over the hollandaise and serve.

Top tip: How to make the perfect poached egg

1. Make sure your eggs are really fresh and at room temperature.
2. The water needs to be as deep as possible. If you can't achieve a rolling boil put the pan to one side of the heat.
3. Salt the water – this reduces the boiling temperature.
4. Add some vinegar to the water – this helps set the protein.
5. Drop the egg into water at a rolling simmer (somewhere in between a simmer and boil), there is no need to swirl. Cook for approximately 2-2½ minutes. Remove with a slotted spoon and press to check it is cooked.

Fried Fish Burrito

This makes a tasty brunch, or if you want to make it into more
of a complete meal you can add Mexican rice as a side order.

Serves 4

Ingredients

- 20g flour (1oz)
- 1 egg
- 100g (3½oz) dried breadcrumbs
- 250g (9oz) fish fillets cut into 4 equal fingers
- Oil for frying
- 1 shallot
- 1 avocado
- Salt
- Chilli sauce
- 1 lime
- 1 head of gem lettuce
- 1 plum tomato
- 2 soft tortilla wraps
- Sour cream
- Pickled chillies or jalapenos to garnish

Method

1. Take three small trays, spread the flour onto the first tray, beat the egg and pour onto the second tray, and put the breadcrumbs on the third.
2. Coat the fish in the flour and pat off the excess, then coat in the egg, drain and finally place into the breadcrumbs.
3. Heat the oil to 180C
4. Take the shallot, peel and finely dice.
5. Cut the avocado in half and remove the stone and skin, slice one half lengthways and mash the other half with a fork before adding a little salt, chilli sauce (to taste) and squeeze of lime.
6. Wash the gem lettuce, removing a couple of leaves for presentation and shred the rest.
7. Dice the plum tomato into ½cm cubes.
8. Warm the tortilla wraps under the grill.
9. Fry or grill the fish fingers until golden, drain and lightly salt.
10. Place the avocado puree onto the wraps, add the shredded lettuce and the diced tomato.
11. Place the sliced avocado at one end of the wrap along with the lettuce leaf. Place the fish fingers on top, squeeze over a little more lime, roll, top with sour cream, chilli sauce, pickled chillies, and serve.

LIVING ON THE EDGE

BEACH LIFE WITH HIDDEN TREATS AND CHAMPAGNE VIEWS

DOWN ON THE FARM, MOBILE POP UPS AND COOL COASTAL LIVING

Mawgan Porth was once the territory of a handful of local surfers and a few tourists who'd strayed out of the surf capital. But since Newquay's reputation has mushroomed and neighbouring Watergate Bay has become synonymous with food and watersports, it's only natural that the attention has been nudged over the headland into nearby Mawgan Porth.

Here towering granite stacks plummet to the flanks of a wide, sandy runway licked by the Atlantic. Turn inland and follow the burbling stream along the valley to St Mawgan, through woods and farmland where roadside stalls and farm shops hint to the abundance of produce that's grown and reared here.

Since the boutique Scarlet Hotel attracted international attention and the Bedruthan Hotel smartened up its act to beckon families seeking eco-luxury, Mawgan Porth has been firmly in the spotlight. BUT FAR FROM THE REALMS OF NEWQUAY'S BEEFED-UP SURF TOWN STATUS, THE STYLE HERE IS STRIPPED BACK AND DOWN TO EARTH.

From pop-up food stalls to fine dining, there's been a foodie awakening here too – and some might say it's been spurred on by Scott Eggleton and Babs Larsen, who accrued a phenomenal reputation when they ran the café at The Park eco holiday village. Now the couple have moved to a new venue at Retorrick Mill, where they are set to blow the farm-to-fork style of feeding to smokin' new levels.

SOCIAL & RUSTIC

{SCOTT AND BABS WOOD FIRED FOOD}

From an outdoor kitchen with off-grid cooking appliances including smoking barrels, an open fire and a clay oven, Scott Eggleton and Babs Larsen are serving up spit roasts, wood-fired pizzas and slow-roasted feasts in a cosy, converted stable block at Retorrick Mill.

Looking every bit a foodie wizard from behind his home-built smoking barrels, Scott says that the only magic to his food is keeping it unfussy and local. **"THE MENU IS MOSTLY DICTATED BY WHAT WE GROW AND REAR,"** he says. He's had pork belly smoking over coals for 18 hours. "Keep the lid on and you keep the moisture and flavours inside, it's not rocket science," he assures me, putting a freshly-kneaded sweet potato and olive focaccia on top of the barrel to prove.

Being situated on Wilf Williams' farm, there is little excuse to source many ingredients beyond its 45 acres. With pigs chomping away alongside the semi-wild gardens, bacon and pork have always featured on the menu. And now Wilf is breeding hardy North Devon and Dexter cows, soon beef will too. Then there are free-range chickens laying eggs and being fattened up for the spit-roast. "We'll be almost meat self-sufficient," declares Scott,

"other than the sustainable game and locally-caught fish that we buy in." They don't have to go far for other ingredients either: "My mum's taking over the poly-tunnel and growing all our veggies and herbs," says Scott, "and the rest of our leaves and veg we get from Gluvian Organics, less than five minutes' walk away." There's also an orchard bursting with apples, pears and cherries.

In a sociable and rustic setting, food is served banquet-style and diners take a seat in converted barns decked out with candles, fairy lights and up-cycled furniture. On weekends the vibe is all about tucking into wood-fired pizzas or pulled pork baps while enjoying a local band or kicking back on sofas around the fire pit. But there are more food adventures in the pipeline such as 'hammocks and hampers' in the orchard, and lantern walks through the woods to dig up slow-roasted pig for dinner.

Although this country lifestyle sounds

worlds away from the coast, Retorrick Mill is a short walk from Mawgan Porth beach and engrained in the coastal lifestyle.

"MANY OF OUR INGREDIENTS COME FROM IN AND AROUND THE OCEAN," says Scott. "We catch a lot of mackerel off the kayak, go spear fishing, catch crabs and go mussel picking. People can even bring their own fish and we'll cook it for them."

Beach life doesn't only influence the food – it's what brought Scott and Babs to Cornwall. Starting his trade under the tutelage of Marco Pierre White and Michel Roux, and working his way through high profile restaurants such as Babington House, Scott confesses he got fed up of cooking for 'middle-class toffs'. So the couple travelled the world, cooking on yachts and island-hopping around Malaysia and Bali.

Eventually lured to Cornwall to help with the set-up of The Park, the couple got hooked on the surf and lifestyle in Mawgan Porth. When Scott's not cooking he's surfing, and Babs can be found walking the dogs on the coast path. "I'm a lot more relaxed about cooking now," says Scott – "hence why I'm working in a barn." If

it's a relaxed attitude we have to thank for the incredible food being served in this informal ambience, perhaps it's time for other high-calibre chefs to take a leaf out of Scott's book and chill out. "We want people to relax, eat dinner and get drunk. It's the sort of place where it's not unusual to start with a good meal and end up dancing on the tables," the happy couple conclude.

Harissa Smoked Pheasant with Pork Belly

We love this dish because the belly and bird go brilliantly together and it's a good autumnal dish with a bit of a kick!

Ingredients

- 1 plucked and drawn (gutted) pheasant
- 1 pork belly
- 3 tbsp brown sugar
- 2 tbsp red wine vinegar

For the dry rub:

- 2 tbsp cumin seeds
- 2 tbsp fennel seeds
- 2 tbsp coriander seeds (all seeds pre-toasted)
- 1 tbsp sea salt
- 1 tbsp dry chilli flakes
- 1 tbsp black peppercorns
- 5 tbsp smoked paprika

Method

1. Chuck all seasoning ingredients into a pestle and grind into a lovely rub for the pork belly. Take the skin off the pork belly and cut it for the dry rub to hold on to. Ideally leave overnight to soak in.
2. We like to slow roast pork belly at 140C in the smoker barrels for 8-12 hours. Or you can oven roast it at 200C for 20 minutes, then cover in foil and cook for another 2 hours at 160C.

For the Harissa sauce:

- 2 chillis
- 1 pepper
- 1 red onion
- 1 garlic bulb

We make our own Harissa sauce in our big barrel smokers. Set the drum (or your oven) to 180C and leave the veggies overnight to roast slowly. Obviously it gets less hot as the coals and wood burn down overnight, so in a domestic fan oven it should only take 20 minutes at 200C.

When these are ready, peel the skins and remove the seeds. Then put into a blender and add:

- 1 tsp toasted cumin seeds
- 1 tsp toasted coriander seeds
- 2 tbsp smoked paprika

For the pheasant dish:

3. Marinate the pheasant in the Harrisa sauce for 8 hours (if you want a bit more of a kick to it).
4. We BBQ'd ours in the barrels but in a domestic oven you could roast it on a high temp at 220 degrees until golden.
5. Then turn down to 180 for about 20 minutes, take the pheasant out and let it rest for 5 minutes. Make a cut on the inside of the leg to check its done. The leg of the pheasant should be a bit pink inside with clear running juices.
6. Carve and mix with the cooked pork. Serve with roasted root vegetables.

Whole Roast Sea Bass with Orange, Bay Leaves, Pink Grapefruit and Fennel

This fish dish is great for sharing – and you can dunk fresh bread into all the tasty juices.

Ingredients
- I kg (2lb 3oz) whole sea bass
- 1 grapefruit
- 1 orange
- 5 fresh bay leaves
- 100g (3½oz) butter
- Olive oil for drizzling
- Handful of fennel seeds
- Sea salt

Method
1. Scale, gut and trim the fins from the fish, and slash 5 times down one side.
2. Make a 'boat' using tinfoil to catch all the juices, drizzle with olive oil and place the fish into it.
3. Season the fish with sea salt and sprinkle with fennel seeds. Peel the zest from the orange and grapefruit and place on top. Poke the bay leaves into the slashes on the fish with chunks of butter.
4. Drizzle olive oil over the fish and squeeze the juices from the citrus fruits all over it.
5. Put it into a pre-warmed oven at 200C for 10 minutes then remove and baste.
6. Pop it back in for another 10 minutes then take it out and let it rest for at least 5 more minutes before serving with fresh bread.

Olive, Sweet Potato and Rosemary Focaccia

This bread is super-tasty and practically a meal on its own.

Ingredients
- 3 sweet potatoes
- 3 cloves garlic
- A handful of soft rosemary tips
- 1kg (2lb 3oz) strong white flour
- 20g (1oz) fresh yeast
- 20g (1oz) Cornish rock salt
- 570ml (1pt) warm water
- 285ml (½pt) olive oil

Plus a handful each of: sea salt, pumpkin seeds, sunflower seeds, to sprinkle on top.

Method

1. Peel and chop the sweet potatoes into 2cm-ish cubes. Drizzle with oil and roast in the oven with the chopped garlic cloves until soft (200C for about 10 minutes).
2. Put all dry ingredients (flour, rock salt, yeast) in a bowl and mix on a slow speed in a mixer using a dough hook. Then add all the liquids (only half of the olive all) and mix slowly for 15 minutes. Then mix on a fast speed for 5 minutes to stretch the gluten (the dough should look shiny by now). Add the sweet potato and garlic and mix for another 2 minutes.
3. Take out the mixed dough and knead into a rugby ball shape, then squash out onto a grease-proofed baking tray and leave for 30 minutes.
4. With a wet finger, poke holes into the bread then stuff with olives and rosemary. Drizzle more olive oil on to it, then sprinkle with the seeds and a good amount of sea salt.
5. Cover lightly with cling film and leave in a warmish place for 30 minutes until doubled in size.
6. Pop into a hot oven (220C) for 10 minutes, then turn down the oven to 200C and turn the tray. Cook for another 20 minutes. Tip: Before putting the dough in, chuck a few ice cubes directly into the bottom of the oven to create a bit of steam – it makes the crust amazing!
7. When it's ready put it on a cooling rack and drizzle with more oil, and when it's cool enough put it in your belly. Yum!

Hot Sticky Toffee Apple Cheesecake

For the base:

- 70g (2½oz) digestive biscuits
- 70g (2½oz) amaretti biscuits
- 70g (2½oz) gingernut biscuits
- 100g (3½oz) melted butter

Smash up the biscuits, add the melted butter and smooth into the base of a dish. It can be a thick base or thin, however you prefer. Pop in the fridge to cool and set.

For the cheese topping:

- 550g (19½oz) cream cheese
- 100g (3½oz) icing sugar
- 150g (5½oz) double cream
- 1 vanilla pod (just the seeds from the pod)

Mix together and layer on top of the biscuit base then pop back into the fridge.

For the sticky toffee apple sauce:

- 5 cooking apples chopped into 1cm-ish cubes
- 10g (⅓oz) butter
- 100g (3½oz) sugar
- 50ml (2fl oz) of a local cider apple brandy (optional)

Melt the sugar and butter in a thick-based pan until it blends into a caramel. Add the brandy and the apple dices. Cook until the apples are barely soft and leave to cool slightly. Pour directly over the cheesecake. It's best to cut the cheesecake into portions and pop into bowls to catch the sauce.

SCOTT'S TIPS FOR SMOKING YOUR OWN FOOD

MAKING A SMOKER

Scott's smoking barrels (also known as Ugly Duck Smokers) are made from 55-gallon drums with fire baskets in the base, and fitted with a thermometer and airflow valves. However, you can make a very basic smoker out of a metal biscuit tin: Use a hammer and nails to perforate the base, fill it halfway with wood chips, put a couple of holes in the lid of the tin, and put it on the heat source (low-heat on the hob or barbecue). Once there is a decent amount of smoke add your meat on a gauze or grill inside the tin.

Smoking can transform even the toughest, cheapest cuts of meat into tender, wonderful feasts. Beef brisket, pork shoulder and ribs are all great on the smoker, as the process melts the fat and breaks down connective tissue, tenderising and flavouring the meat.

PERFECT SMOKING

Meat should be smoked for at least 30 minutes per pound, sometimes longer. Try to keep the temperature of your smoker constant – don't be tempted to open the lid as this keeps the heat, and the flavour, in. For a ballpark idea of how long to cook your particular type of meat, compare different recipes; you can also use a digital probe to monitor the temperature of your smoker.

TUCK IN

The trick is to get the meat to fall off the bone, without overcooking it. You should be able to pull a good chunk of it away with a fork with no resistance, but the meat should still be full of fat and moisture. The cooked meat should be left to stand for at least 10 minutes before tucking in.

Salt Water
IN THE AIR
AND
Adventure
IN MY SOUL

CORNISH STREET FOOD

Mobile foodie vans are serving lashings of excellent Cornish street food in handy locations all over the county. The Laid Back Coffee Co. and Wild Bake are two of these pop-up food shacks collaborating on beachside brunches in Mawgan Porth and beyond.

{WILD BAKE}

Lewis and Claire Cole set up the Wild Bake pizza trailer so that their work would fit around their love of the beach and time with their three children.

"FOOD IS A BIT LIKE LIFE – LESS IS MORE. We wanted a more simple life, and more time on the beach with our children," says Claire. It was in France that the couple came across the trend of pizza vans visiting campsites and beaches. Being an eco-conscious couple, instead of copying the electric ovens they saw on the Continent, they went down the route of having a mobile wood-fired oven. "The oven is incredibly heavy – about the same weight as the average horse – which is how we ended up with a unique horsebox as our vehicle. Also we needed something we could easily tow around the Cornish lanes to offbeat locations," says Lewis.

Touring beaches, campsites and town spots, Wild Bake serves up rustic, wood-fired pizzas topped with fresh Cornish ingredients. As well as staple classics, they create seasonal specials such as the Padstow Estuary pizza topped with Porthilly mussels, sea aster, sea purslane and sea spinach sourced from around the Camel Estuary.

WOOD FIRED STREET FOOD

Wild Bake's Breakfast Pizza

Ingredients

- 800g (1lb 12oz) pizza dough
- 200ml (7fl oz) pizza sauce
- 400g (14oz) mozzarella and mature cheddar mix
- 4 cooked Cornish sausages
- 6 rashers smoked streaky bacon, cut in to strips
- 200g (7oz) chestnut mushrooms, sliced
- 200g (7oz) cherry tomatoes, halved
- 2tsp dried oregano
- 20ml – or a good drizzle – Mrs Middleton's rapeseed oil

Wild Bake Pizza Dough:

- 1kg of 00 grade flour
- 600ml (1pt) cold water
- 4tsp salt
- ½ tsp fresh yeast

Combine all the ingredients in a large bowl. Then knead for 15 minutes.

Wild Bake Pizza Sauce:

- 1 tin peeled plum tomatoes
- Handful basil leaves
- 2 cloves garlic
- Sea salt and cracked black pepper to season

Blitz together until smooth. (This sauce is also great for pasta – such as bolognese or lasagne.)

Method

1. Let the dough prove for 3 hours in a warm room, knock the dough back and divide into 200g portions.
2. Roll the portions into balls then leave to prove again for further 2 hours.
3. Preheat oven to its highest setting.
4. Roll or stretch the balls out and place them on baking trays lined with baking paper.
5. Cover the bases with the pizza sauce using the back of a spoon, leaving an inch border around the edge. Sprinkle the cheese evenly then scatter the sausage, bacon, mushrooms and cherry tomatoes over each pizza.
6. Top them with a pinch of oregano and bake in the oven for around 20 minutes or until the cheese has started to crisp and the crust has turned golden brown and risen.
7. Just before you serve, drizzle the pizza with some really nice oil – we use Mrs Middleton's rapeseed oil (she also has infused oils like basil or chilli that go down a treat!)

Tip: For best results use a ceramic pizza stone preheated in the oven.

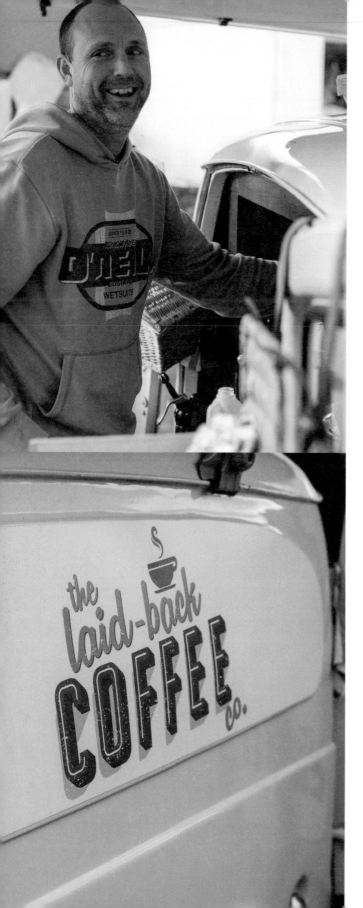

COFFEE & CAKE

{THE LAID BACK COFFEE CO.}

Rosie and Graham Hoppe serve freshly-ground Origin coffee and home-baked cakes from the back of their 1969 Morris Minor Van. "We just wanted to do something that meant we could enjoy more family time and make the most of the beach life on our doorstep," explains Rosie. Mawgan Porth is their main pitch, where the couple also spend an awful lot of their time on the beach with their two girls.

Having been a chef in Sydney, Perth and Auckland, where the café culture is more sophisticated than here in the UK, Graham was keen to latch on to the growing taste for good coffee back here in Britain. He does all the baking for the van, bringing influences from all over the world into the cakes and pastries served. "We might have anything from chocolate brownies to 'rugelach' – an Eastern European pastry made from vanilla dough, nuts, chocolate, fruit and apricot jam," he says.

Both keen surfers BC (Before Children), Graham and Rosie may have put the sport on the backburner while the kids are young, but they are still avid beach goers. "For now I SUP (Stand Up Paddleboard) and I'll get back to surfing more when the girls have grown up," says Graham. "The tide goes in and out. Storms come and go. There will always be waves. For now I'm busy enjoying life in Cornwall."

Orange, Almond and Olive Oil Cake

- 2 large, unwaxed (or scrubbed under a hot tap) oranges
- 100ml extra virgin olive oil
- 175g (6oz) caster sugar
- 4 free-range eggs
- 175g (6oz) ground almonds
- 2 tsp baking powder

- Line and oil an 8-inch round tin and pre-heat the oven to 180C.
- Put the oranges in a pan of water, bring to the boil and gently simmer for 30 mins.
- Cut the fruit into quarters. Remove the pips and put the skin and pulp of one orange in a blender along with the skin of the second orange. Blitz until smooth.
- Whisk the oil, sugar and eggs until light.
- Gently fold in the almonds and baking powder.
- Fold in the fruit and spoon into the tin.
- Bake for 50-60 mins until golden and risen.

SUNDOWNER COCKTAILS

{SCARLET HOTEL}

Kick back on the terrace at The Scarlet – it's the perfect spot for a sundowner with stunning sea views. Try a mojito or an Espresso martini – two of the classic cocktails served here.

Mojito

This mojito recipe is extra zingy and refreshing – ideal for a long, hot summer's evening:

- 35ml white rum
- 35ml soda water
- 1½ limes
- 7 mint leaves
- 35ml brown sugar

Crush the sugar and mint in a sturdy highball glass. Juice the limes and pour into the glass. Fill with crushed ice. Add the rum and soda water, stir. Garnish with a mint sprig and lime wedges.

Espresso Martini

This indulgent espresso martini will give you an intense kick:

- 35ml Black Cow vodka
- 25ml Zuidam Café Liqueur
- 25ml espresso coffee
- 25ml sugar syrup
- 3 coffee beans

Fill your cocktail shaker with ice cubes. Add all the ingredients then shake until cold. Strain into a stemmed martini glass. Garnish with coffee beans.

BUZZING SURF TOWN

HIP WITH HEALTH, AND A SMATTERING OF FOODIE WEALTH

FROM SURF CAPITAL TO GASTRONOMIC HOT SPOT

Britain's unofficial surf capital, in recent years Newquay has become popular for its world-class waves and laid-back beach lifestyle. Yet it was back in Victorian times that the area was established as one of the UK's most popular holiday resorts – its rugged coast, perfect beaches and rolling waves pulling the bucket and spade brigades long before surfers came to town.

From Fistral beach – hailed as one of the best surf breaks in the country – to 'The Wedge' at Tolcarne, there are waves to suit every level of surfer, and there's no shortage of surf shops and surf schools to cater for the masses of board riders that flock here. Flaunting a surf-by-day, party-by night attitude, there has always been a vibrant après surf scene in town too.

However, like the original surfing generation, Newquay is growing up and a more sophisticated nightlife is emerging: people are sipping sundowners by the sea, chilling out in stylish wine bars and dining on fresh, local food. Instead of partying till sunrise, the new wave of surfers are more likely to get up with the sun and paddle out for a dawny, before a smoothie and a big breakfast by the beach.

IN LINE WITH THIS FRESH, ENERGETIC VIBE IN TOWN, THE FOODIE SCENE IS CHANGING TOO. No longer falling back on the seaside staple of fish and chips, restaurants are drawing on the abundance of Cornish produce and using local ingredients to create globally influenced menus. Being a historic fishing port it's only natural that seafood is still in the spotlight, with all sorts of fresh fish being flipped straight from the fishing boats and into the frying pans of talented local chefs.

HEALTHY GOODNESS

{JAM JAR}

A couple of years ago Elsie Pinniger opened the Jam Jar café with Jess Davis, creating a cosy hangout where surfers can enjoy locally roasted coffee and delicious home-baking on their way to and from the town beaches. Passionate about food and wanting to provide a more extensive menu than the space at the Jam Jar could accommodate, Elsie has recently expanded into a new venture – Gilmore's – where she'll continue dishing up legendary fare to Newquay's foodies and surfers.

Having taken the helm at the Jam Jar, Jess is maintaining the healthy laid back vibe, serving fresh and nutritious food and drinks alongside organic coffee – from homemade granola and breakfast smoothies for breakfast, to almond milk flat whites, toasted avo bagels and gluten-free brownies. Proud of her healthy baking, Jess has made it her purpose in life to incorporate her passion for making cakes with her interest in nutrition and fitness.

"I'VE BEEN BAKING GLUTEN-FREE CAKES FOR A WHILE NOW BUT MORE RECENTLY I'M DOING DAIRY FREE, REFINED SUGAR FREE AND EVEN RAW CAKES! I like the idea that people can go out with friends for a treat and not leave feeling guilty, but nourished and full of energy," she says.

HEALTHY BREAKFAST SMOOTHIES

Kick-start your day with one of these healthy, delicious smoothies.

Green Smoothie

Avocados and coconut are not only great for both your hair and skin, but internally they can lower your blood sugar too. They also help to improve brain function, making this the perfect mid-morning boost. Spirulina is packed with protein, vitamins and minerals, helping to detoxify the body – ideal after a long weekend of fun!

1 ripe avocado
1 banana, preferably frozen
Handful washed spinach
1 tsp spirulina
1 tsp organic virgin coconut oil
500ml coconut water

Banana Pecan Smoothie

Maca powder is a Peruvian root that helps to improve stamina and energy levels, and pecans are jam-packed with vitamin E to make your skin glow. Bananas are high in potassium, and cinnamon (like the banana) is a mood enhancer. So: what's not to love? This is the perfect start to any day.

1 banana, preferably frozen
3 medjool dates
Small handful raw pecan nuts
1 tsp maca powder
500ml milk of choice (I use organic almond milk)
Pinch of cinnamon to decorate

SMOOTHIES

4.50

1 Early Bird
GLUTEN FREE OATS, BANANA, HONEY, OAT MILK, CINNAMON, YOGHURT, MACA

2 CLEAN GREEN
AVOCADO, SPINACH, BANANA, ALMOND MILK, SPIRULINA

DF

3 BERRY GLOW
RASPBERRIES, BLUEBERRIES, MAPLE SYRUP, YOGHURT, CHIA SEEDS

4 BOUNTY Bliss
COCONUT MILK, BANANA, COCONUT OIL, AGAVE NECTAR

DF

5 LEMON Drizzle
LEMON, HONEY, MINT, YOGHURT, BEE POLLEN

6 BIG BOY
PEANUT BUTTER, BANANA, ALMOND MILK, SESAME SEEDS, WHEY PROTEIN

DF

DAIRY FREE
EL OF THE DAY!

ORGANIC

CHOOSE FROM:
SKIMMED/WHOLE

DOUBL
MACC
AMERI
FLAT V
CAPPU
MOCHA
ICED C
HOT CH
DELUXE
CHAI L

BUTTER
DOUBLE ESP

COLD B
SLOW DRIP

RAWSO
ORGANIC RAW

WHY GLUTEN FREE?

Jess explains why baking without wheat flour doesn't have to take the spring out of your cake, but can put a spring back in your step:

"I bake gluten-free cakes because people are becoming more in tune with their bodies and the types of foods that make them feel good. I don't like to preach about what people should eat, I just believe you should eat things that make you feel good inside and out. As with many people, I find that gluten (particularly wheat) makes me feel bloated and sluggish, so I avoid it wherever possible. So if you can make a perfectly delicious cake without the addition of processed wheat, then why not? These days I also make dairy-free cakes for vegans and people with lactose intolerances, and I'm coming up with new recipes for sugar-free cakes for the super healthy cake lover!"

Gluten free Raspberry and Almond Frangipan Loaf

Ingredients

- 200g (7oz) soft butter
- 200g (7oz) unrefined golden caster sugar
- 200g (7oz) ground almonds
- 150g (5.3oz) Doves organic gluten-free self raising flour
- Few drops almond oil
- 4 free-range eggs
- 200g (7oz) fresh raspberries or other seasonal berries
- 50g (1.7oz) flaked almonds
- Icing sugar to decorate

Method

1. Preheat your oven to 170C and line a loaf tin with baking paper.
2. Beat together the soft butter and sugar until pale and fluffy.
3. Gradually add the eggs one at a time until fully incorporated.
4. Sift in the flour and ground almonds.
5. Fold in the fresh raspberries and pour into your lined tin.
6. Scatter over the flaked almonds and bake for approximately 40 minutes until it's risen and golden and a knife comes out clean when you insert it into the cake.
7. Once cooled dust over icing sugar and serve with more fresh berries and Rodda's clotted cream!

Jess's Dark Chocolate and Beetroot Cake
(Dairy, gluten and refined sugar free)

Ingredients
- 100g (3.5oz) raw cacao powder (or cocoa is fine)
- 100g (3.5oz) gluten free self-raising flour
- 200g (7oz) raw beetroot, peeled and grated
- 200g (7oz) ground almonds
- 200ml (.35 pt) virgin coconut oil, melted
- 200g (7oz) raw coconut sugar
- 3 free-range eggs
- Seeds of 1 vanilla bean pod

Method
1. Preheat your oven to 160C and grease your bundt tin with a little oil.
2. Whisk the eggs, coconut sugar, melted coconut oil and vanilla beans until frothy and light.
3. Add grated beetroot and ground almonds and mix well.
4. Sift in the flour and baking powder and fold through.
5. Pour mixture into your tin and bake for 40 minutes. It will have a nice dark glossy finish once baked. Make sure you turn it out whilst it's still warm (not hot) or else it will get stuck! This cake is so nutritious you could eat it for breakfast!

THROW A DIVINE DINNER PARTY!

{ELSIE & DEB'S WINE NIGHTS}

While Newquay is infamous for its stag and hen weekends, these days it's also becoming known for a more sophisticated social scene – including swanky cocktail evenings and wine nights at boutique bars. Embracing the changing face of Newquay's food and drink scene, Elsie Pinniger teamed up with wine buff Debbie Warner to launch the Wine Club, providing an alternative evening out in Newquay. "Cooking for friends and enjoying food and drink is my ideal way of spending time with people," says Elsie. "I don't really go out and get drunk in town anymore, I'd rather have friends round, and that's what we try and recreate here – the ambience of having people round to your house," she explains. With just 12 or so diners tucking into five courses in each sitting, it really does feel as if you've crashed a very cool dinner party.

Each evening is based on wines from a particular region or country, and as Debbie flips open the wine atlas and passes round books and maps, talk around the table inevitably turns to travel. "I try to cover areas that aren't typically known for the amazing wines they produce, and introduce people to varieties they wouldn't typically opt for in a bar or supermarket," says Debbie, who has racked up a long list of wine qualifications and worked as a sommelier at Fifteen Cornwall. "People are quick to go into a bar and order a Sauvignon Blanc, but an Austrian Grüner would be an amazing alternative, with the big fruit hit of a Sauvignon Blanc yet with more interesting savoury notes and white pepper too," she says.

Elsie matches the food to Debbie's wine selection, and although the dishes are tailored to wine regions around the world, seasonal ingredients are key in her

cooking. "We get loads of our produce from veg boxes and from our gardens," Elsie says. "I was brought up in a household where everything was grown in the garden and cooked from scratch. When convenience food came around it was a time saving revelation for my mum's generation, but no one really bothered to stop and think what was in it. We still don't know the consequences of what goes in processed and fast food, but people are starting to become more educated about food now. I'm always baffled by people who aren't fussed about food.

COOKING – AND KNOWING WHAT'S IN THINGS WE EAT – IS SOMETHING THAT EVERYONE SHOULD KNOW."

"In summer we might have Spanish wines served with fresh mackerel caught by our friends, or Italian wines paired with fresh pasta tossed with fresh vegetables from our gardens," says Debbie. "And in winter we go for cooler, more mountainous regions such as Austria and Hungary. A lot of people think Hungarian wines are typically very sweet, because the region of Tokaj was known for producing one of the world's most famous sweet wines, but since the fall of Communism wineries have been free to experiment and there is now

excellent quality dry Tokaj being produced there," she explains. "This dry Hungarian Tokaj pairs well with Elsie's smoked fish mousse, because it's fermented and aged in oak, which works with the flavour of the smoked fish. It is also great with barbecued food because of its smoky tones."

Working your way from a sparkling Pinot Grigio to a flagship Austrian Grüner, you can learn a huge amount about different parts of the world through the food and wine served by Elsie and Debbie. But what these wine nights – and their popularity – also prove, is that Newquay's foodie scene is indeed changing. "People are starting to take back their time and see food as pleasure, not just as fuel. We aim to make quality food and wine much more accessible, by keeping our prices low and serving it in a really informal structure," the girls conclude.

TIPS FOR GETTING PICKLED

Debbie makes homemade pickles to go with the food Elsie serves at the Wine Club, so we asked her a bit more about the art of pickling. It used to be just WI members and grannies that made their own jams and pickles – when preserving used to be a genuine way of making the surplus of food grown in summer last through the winter months – but as people start to grow more of their own produce again we're retrieving a passion for making our own preserves too.

• **The pickling process usually takes at least two weeks.** However, pickled cucumbers – or gherkins – can be ready within 24 hours and taste much better than buying a jar of gherkins from the supermarket. Onions, on the other hand, need to be left for weeks in the pickling liquor until they are ready to eat.

• **Debbie's pickling liquors are all based on cider vinegar, white wine vinegar and sugar.** Typically you need about twice as much vinegar as sugar, but you can taste the pickling liquor and adjust accordingly.

• **You can season your pickling liquor with whatever herbs and seasoning complement the produce you are pickling.** In cucumber pickling liquor Debbie combines dill, honey, peppercorns, chilli flakes and mustard seeds. For carrots she uses fennel and caraway seeds. And for onions, she uses star anise, coriander seeds and onion seeds.

• **To make easy pickled cucumbers simply slice your cucumbers lengthways and put them into a jar.** Boil up your pickling liquor (cider vinegar, white wine vinegar, sugar, dill, honey, peppercorns, chilli flakes and mustard seeds), pour over the cucumber and seal the jar. Within 24 hours you've got the perfect accompaniment to homemade burgers!

THE PERFECT FINGER FOOD

Pork Schnitzel

Schnitzels make great finger food and go well with sparkling wine or Champagne. To make a vegetarian version replace the pork with aubergine.

Per person

Ingredients
- 200g (7oz) pork (we use pork thigh as it's a bit more fatty) / or aubergine for veggie
- 250g (9oz) plain flour
- ½ white loaf (stale)
- 1 egg

Method
1. If going for the veggie option first of all slice the aubergine into centimetre-thick discs and sprinkle with salt. Leave for an hour or so to get the moisture out. Then follow the steps below.
2. Cut the pork into medallions then bash until it's thin. Season the pork.
3. Make the breadcrumbs by blitzing the stale bread in a blender.
4. Beat the egg and leave to one side. In another dish put the plain flour.
5. Coat the pork in the flour, dip in egg, then dip in the breadcrumbs.
6. Heat vegetable oil in a deep fat fryer or deep saucepan. Fry the pork in small batches until golden brown.
7. Serve with a good artisan ketchup like Kernow Ketchup.

Fennel and Celeriac Salad with Orange Dressing

Serves 6

Ingredients
- 1 celeriac
- 3 fennel bulbs
- Bunch of thyme
- 150g (5oz) butter
- 200g (7oz) whole hazelnuts

Dressing:
- 100ml (4fl oz) olive oil
- 50ml (2fl oz) white wine vinegar
- 1 tsp brown sugar
- 1 orange, juice of
- Salt and pepper

Method
1. Peel and chop the celeriac into centimetre cubes. Chop the fennel into sixths.
2. Arrange the celeriac and fennel on a baking tray with thyme, a dash of olive oil and cubes of butter, and roast for 30 minutes at 200C. Leave to cool
3. Toast the hazelnuts in a frying pan.
4. To make the dressing shake all the ingredients in a jar, with extra seasoning to taste.
5. Crush the hazelnuts into broken bits.
6. On a serving board arrange a mix of watercress, spinach and your favourite leaves.
7. Arrange the roast fennel and celeriac. Sprinkle over the hazelnuts and dressing, and it's ready to serve.

Salmon Mousse

This salmon mousse is a really good starter –
quick and easy to make and super tasty. It
pairs wonderfully with a mineral wine.

Serves 6

Ingredients

- 250g (8oz) joint of salmon
- 250g (8oz) smoked salmon
  (or you can use trout or
  mackerel)
- 125g (4½oz) cream cheese
- 50ml double cream
- Bunch of dill
- ½ lemon, juiced
- ½pt milk
- Salt and pepper to season

Method

1. Poach the joint of salmon
   in a pan of milk. Once it's
   cooked take it out and leave
   to cool.
2. Put the cooled salmon and
   all the rest of the ingredients
   into a blender, plus half of the
   dill. Blend until smooth.
3. Roughly chop the rest of the
   dill and mix in.
4. Place in a ramekin dish and
   put in the fridge until ready to
   serve. It's great with toasted
   rye bread.

Chestnut and Brandy Semifreddo with Chocolate Ganache

This is a delicious dessert – like soft ice cream

Ingredients
- 2 tins of chestnut purée (we use Merchant Gourmet)
- 300ml double cream
- 3 tbsp brandy
- 100g (3½oz) caster sugar

Ganache:
- 400g (14oz) dark chocolate
- 250ml (9fl oz) double cream

Method
1. Combine the chestnut purée, double cream, brandy and caster sugar in a blender until well combined.
2. Pour into a shallow flat tray or individual dishes. Line with cling film and put into the freezer until almost frozen.
3. Take out after an hour so it has the consistency of soft ice cream.
4. To make the ganache, heat the cream in a saucepan, making sure you don't boil it. Then chop the chocolate into pieces and slowly stir it into the cream until it's all melted. Leave to set.
5. Scoop it out with an ice cream scoop and serve on top of the chestnut base, topped with Chantilly cream.

Meat And Cheese Raclette with Homemade Pickles

We've used a raclette grill but you can easily do this on a barbecue using foil

Ingredients

- 500g (1lb 2oz) potatoes
- Cured meat
- Cheese

Method

1. Boil the potatoes until just cooked and set aside.
2. Use a selection of your favourite cured meats like chorizo and serrano ham, combined with nutty, sweet cheese such as Jarlesberg, Emmental or Gouda.
3. Heat the raclette grill and put the potatoes on first, then place the meat and cheese on your tray. (If you're doing it on a barbecue simply place the ingredients on tin foil).
4. Remove the potatoes once they start to go golden, the meats once they are sizzling and the cheese as it starts to go gooey.
5. Serve with bread and pickles.

NEW WAVE

NEWQUAY'S COOL NEW FOODIE PLACES

Thanks to a new wave of restaurants mixed in with its traditional
seaside eateries, Newquay's shedding its party image and becoming
something of a gourmet hotspot. Here are five new restaurants leading
the foodie crusade:

◼ FSC SURF DINER, CLIFF ROAD

Overlooking the surf rolling into Newquay Bay, this American-style diner (situated above the Fistral Surf Co) has already become a firm favourite for its homemade burgers, locally-sourced steaks and real sausage hot dogs. Not only is the food a hit but you also can't beat the cool, surfside setting of this retro-style diner decked out with authentic Americana.
www.fistralsurfco.co.uk/diner

◼ BUSH PEPPER, FORE STREET

Serving the likes of kangaroo and crocodile, this original Aussie-style restaurant combines the finest ingredients from Cornwall and Australia in a globally-influenced menu. Australian owner and chef Chris Brookes has a tangible passion for food and creates healthy and exotic dishes, from seafood and succulent meat platters to vegetarian options.
www.bushpepper.co.uk

◼ THE STABLE, FISTRAL BEACH

No ordinary pizza restaurant, the emphasis at The Stable is on delicious, local ingredients served with a view over the UK's most iconic surf beach. Pizzas are piled high with fresh, seasonal toppings on organic sourdough bases, and as an alternative there are handcrafted pies too. In addition to good food, the cider alone is worth coming here for, with an ever-changing list of over 80 varieties – most of which hail from the West Country.
www.stablepizza.com

◼ GUSTO, SOUTH QUAY HILL

Inspired by a medley of countries from Morocco and Greece to Italy and Spain, Simon Evans dishes out tasty salad boxes and unique takeaway dishes big in flavour, from his Deli Bar above Newquay harbour. From the baked falafels and seasonal salads, to Sunday roast dinners in a bag, the hearty dishes make the perfect nosebag for surfers, walkers and beach lovers to take home or enjoy by the sea.
Facebook page: Gusto-deli-Bar

◼ GILMORE'S, TOWER ROAD

Elsie Pinniger recently opened Gilmore's café to provide a cosy hangout close to Fistral Beach. Focussing on Californian-Mexican cuisine and healthy eating, Elsie serves up the best tortilla wraps in town and fare that goes hand-in-hand with the Cali lifestyle in Newquay.
Instagram: gilmoresnewquay

TASTY FUSION FOOD WITH AN AUSSIE TWIST

{BUSH PEPPER}

Aussie Chris Brookes spent his early twenties surfing and travelling. Newquay was on his list of destinations and he fell in love with the town, staying for a winter before moving on again. Recently he moved back here with his wife Heather and opened Bush Pepper, offering modern Australian fusion food.

Barramundi with Mango and Chilli Salsa

This is one of my favourite fusion-style seaside dishes. Since I became a chef in Australia 12 years ago I've modified the dish to include some of the lovely fresh produce of Cornwall. Enjoy...

Serves 4
Ingredients

- 4 barramundi or seabass fillets
- Cold pressed rapeseed oil
- 500g (1lb) Cornish new potatoes
- 250g (9oz) Canara Farm organic chard
- 1 lime (for garnish)
- Pea shoots
- 2 tsp sea salt
- Black pepper

Mango Salsa

- 1 mango (1cm diced)
- 1 lime (zested and juiced)
- 1 long red chilli (finely diced)
- 1 tbsp chopped coriander
- 2 tsp white wine vinegar
- 1 tsp sugar

Method

1. Prepare all the salsa ingredients and mix together in a bowl. Allow at least an hour for the flavours to marry.
2. Place the new potatoes in a saucepan, add cold water and 2 teaspoons of salt, bring to the boil and cook till the potatoes are soft in the centre.
3. Remove from water. Put to one side.
4. Reheat the potatoes when ready to serve the rest of the components of the dish. Season with a pinch of sea salt and drizzle with rapeseed oil.
5. Slice chard in 1 cm strips. Blanch in boiling, salted water for 2 minutes then remove from water and refresh in cold iced water. Strain. Put to one side.
6. Reheat the chard in a pan when ready to serve, adding a small amount of cold pressed rapeseed oil and sea salt.
7. Either BBQ or pan fry the barramundi skin side down, with a small amount of cold pressed rapeseed oil.
8. Cook the fish almost all the way through on the skin side as this will allow a crispy skin, then flip and finish cooking
9. When you are about to flip the fish, this is the perfect time to reheat your new potatoes and chard. The whole process should take 5 to 8 minutes depending on the size of the fish

To serve, place the new potatoes and chard in the centre of the plate. Place fish on top, add a spoonful of mango salsa, a wedge of lime and pea shoots to garnish. Drizzle with rapeseed oil.

LAND OF GIANTS

WOODED VALES, SURF CULTURE AND LASHINGS OF COOL COASTAL STYLE

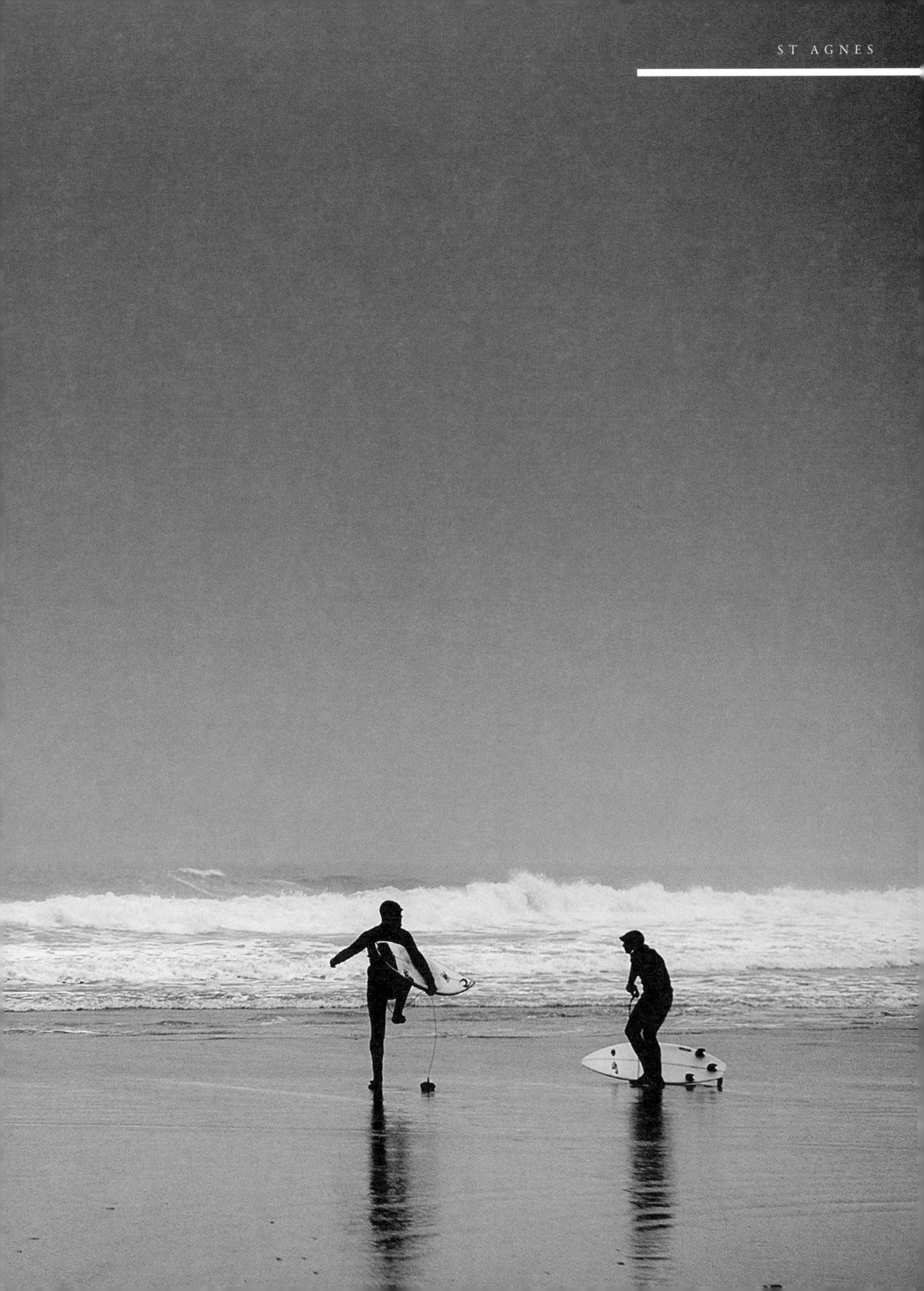

TRADITIONAL MINING TOWN WITH A NEW FOODIE VIBE

St Agnes is a classic Cornish village huddled beside some of the wildest, most rugged coastal land in North Cornwall. Here the dramatic, wave-lashed cliffs are punctuated by abandoned engine houses and mine shafts harking back to the area's prosperous mining heritage. Beneath the towering, gorse-smattered cliffs await sandy coves and a series of surf breaks: Cornwall's legendary 'Badlands'.

Dubbed the 'Badlands' by St Agnes' original surf community of the 1980s, the label was designed to stop new and inexperienced surfers flooding in and taking waves from the locals. And it worked – while nearby breaks became weighted down by holidaymakers and touring surfers, the line-ups at Chapel Porth and Trevaunance Cove were always ruled by talented and experienced locals surfers such as Steve Bunt and Chops Lascelles.

DESPITE AN INFLUX OF OUTSIDERS INTO THE VILLAGE AND THE SURF OVER THE YEARS, A TIGHT-KNIT COMMUNITY STILL REIGNS THE WAVES AND VILLAGE LIFE. However, these days the vibe isn't so hostile to outsiders. After all, it might just be down to the nature of this place that the 'Badlands' were ever conceived: A combination of harsh, unforgiving landscapes, narrow, winding tracks to the sea and gnarly breaks that dictate you need to be a decent surfer to catch a wave. And if you earn your place in the line-up, pad along the beaches, take a hike along the cliff tops or follow the valley that meanders inland to fertile farmland, then you'll see that this isn't really the 'Badlands' at all.

PROPER CORNISH WELCOME

{NO.4}

Serving homemade choc ices and a unique twist on 'surf and turf,' the menu at No.4 echoes the beach life on its doorstep.

In a Cornish love story that started with food, Nola Kinna and Adam Vasey met in St Agnes, where Adam's mum ran Schooners restaurant and Nola came to work when she was sixteen. More than a decade later they set up No.4 in the village where they met. The duo's love of food and their surroundings has inspired a daily-changing menu that teams Cornish-reared meats and locally caught seafood with bold, seasonal flavours.

"WE LIKE TO PAIR THE COAST AND THE COUNTRYSIDE THROUGH OUR FOOD," says Nola. "We're not a typical beach-style diner, but nevertheless our menus reflect the Cornish coastal lifestyle. The monktail and crispy short rib dish (pictured) is our take on surf and turf. Or you might have pork rib eye with cockles. Or scallops with crispy belly pork. We're trying to push people's conceptions of food, but we're not upmarket and fussy. We just like to use simple, honest food and make it a bit different," she says.

Having grown up in his mum's restaurant, chef Adam knows exactly where to get his hands on the best local ingredients. "Most of our suppliers are close to home. We get leaves from Manic Organic in Porthtowan, pork from Primrose Herd and steak from Philip Warren – because it's got the best aging room in Cornwall. A lot of our fish is landed by friends with fishing boats and is still flapping when it's delivered to our door. We love Cornish produce, but we won't use Cornish for the sake of it – it's got to be a kick-ass product," Adam says.

Massively influenced by the restaurant's location, Adam not only loves the coastline for its surf and mining heritage, but also for its abundance of wild ingredients that he can use in his cooking: samphire for fish dishes, gorse flowers for salads, three-cornered leeks to pair

with pork, and wild garlic that goes wonderfully with his gnocchi. The drinks cabinet is inspired by the surroundings as well; alongside Tarquin's Gin distilled in Cornwall and artisan ales brewed in Penryn, you'll find Nola's blackberry gin and sloe fizz made from foraged berries.

For all its meticulous sourcing and immaculately presented platefuls, No.4 is far from stuffy and upmarket. In the shabby-chic dining room you'd be just as happy in flip-flops and boardies as dressed up in your glad-rags for dinner. "We've known this building since we were kids," Adam explains. "We rent it off one of our best mates (the son of the late legendary surfer and board shaper Chops Lascelles) and we want the local surfers to feel comfy here and be able to afford to come in for a slap-up meal."

The restaurant has attracted a huge local following for its feast nights, when all the tables are pushed together and a themed banquet is served. "These nights are all about bringing different people together over unusual food combinations," says Adam. **"BASICALLY, WE'RE JUST BONKERS ABOUT GOOD FOOD, BUT IT DOESN'T HAVE TO BE FANCY.** One of our all time favourite places to eat is Chapel Porth Café,

where you get legendary croque-monsieurs and hedgehog ice creams, slap bang on the beach." What with the signature No.4 Choc Ice (much like a deluxe Snicker's ice cream) becoming a firm favourite and being snapped up nearly as quickly as Chapel Porth's hedgehogs, No.4 is already creating a foodie legend that's sure to go down in history alongside mining and the 'Badlands'.

Scallops and Crispy Pork Belly

Serves 4

Ingredients

Scallops

- 12 Scallops (roe on)
- 100 ml (3½fl oz) Calvados
- 100g (3½oz) unsalted butter
- Pinch of Maldon sea salt

Pork belly

- 1kg (2lbs) pork belly (we use Primrose Herd pork; ask your butcher for the ribs out)
- 3 white onions
- 2 carrots
- 3 sticks of celery
- 1 bottle of cider

Method

1. Place onions, celery, carrots and cider (we use Cornish Orchards) in a roasting tray.
2. Place the pork belly on top of the veg and slow cook for 4 hours.
3. Lift the pork out and press it overnight with something flat and heavy. Once it's pressed cut it up into squares – about the same size as the scallops.
4. Before serving cook off in the oven at full temp (250C) till the fat is crispy on the top.
5. Then flash the scallops in a very hot pan with butter till they're golden on the outside. Add a good pinch of chopped parsley to the butter and serve.

Beetroot Tartar and No4 Ricotta

Serves 4

Ingredients

Ricotta

- 500ml (18fl oz) whole milk
- 500ml (18fl oz) double cream
- Pinch of Maldon sea salt
- 3 lemons, juice of

Beetroot Tartar

- 1kg (2lb) raw beetroot
- 1 banana shallot
- 20g (1oz) capers
- 20g (1oz) cornichons
- 1 tbsp Dijon mustard
- 1 tbsp tomato ketchup
- ½ tbsp Worcestershire sauce
- ½ tsp Tabasco sauce

Salsa Verde

- ½ bunch parsley
- ½ bunch mint
- 1 tsp of red wine vinegar
- 1 tbsp Dijon mustard
- 100 ml (3½fl oz) olive oil

Method

1. For the ricotta, add the whole milk to the double cream and add 2 pinches salt.
2. Heat up to 90F and take off the heat, add the lemon juice, stir and leave for 20 minutes.
3. After 20 minutes, pass though muslin so the curds collect and the whey passes through. Throw the whey away and keep ricotta in the fridge.
4. Take the beetroots and boil for about 30 minutes till your knife goes easily through the middle. Skin them whilst still warm and finely dice into cubes.
5. Very finely dice up the gherkins, capers and shallots, then add Dijon mustard, Tabasco and Worcestershire sauce – mix through the diced beetroot.
6. For the salsa verde, finely chop the mint and parsley, mix with red wine vinegar and Dijon mustard, season and add a slug of good olive oil.
7. Drizzle over the top of the beetroot and ricotta.
8. Serve with croutons.

Monk Tail and Short Rib Nugget

Serves 4

Ingredients

Monk tail
- 4 monkfish tails (200-300g each) double skinned – ask your fishmonger to do this for you
- 250g (9oz) unsalted butter

Short-rib nugget
- 1kg (2lb) beef short-rib
- 3 white onions
- 2 carrots
- 3 sticks of celery
- 1 bottle of ale
- 2 eggs
- 200g (7oz) plain flour
- 200g (7oz) Panko breadcrumbs

Jerusalem artichoke purée
- 500g (17½oz) cleaned Jerusalem artichokes
- 150g (5oz) unsalted butter
- 200ml (7fl oz) double cream
- ½ tsp table salt

Green butter
- 250g (9oz) unsalted butter
- 1 bunch of parsley
- ½ bag of spinach
- ½ lemon
- 2 cloves garlic

Method

1. For the nugget, heavily season the beef short-rib (ask your butcher for Jacobs ladder) and brown off in a pan.
2. Make a braising liquor – add carrots, onion, celery, fennel and garlic into a big oven tray, add in a bottle of good Cornish ale (we use Rebel Brewing Co Cornish Sunset)
3. Put your ribs on the veggies and cover with baking parchment and tin foil. Pop in the oven at 180C for 3½ - 4 hours. Have a cup of tea, or three…
4. Once it's cooked shred the meat and mix with finely diced onion that's been sweated down in a pan. Add enough braising juice to form the mix into little squares, then dip in flour, then beaten egg, then breadcrumbs and deep fry them off just before you serve.
5. For the artichoke purée, peel and chop Jerusalem artichokes and boil until soft. Drain and put back into pan, then add double cream, loads of butter and season. Bring it back up to the boil, purée it through a food processor and then run it through a sieve to get it really smooth and creamy.
6. For the monk tail: the very end of monk tails are the bits people don't usually use, so ask your fishmonger if they can get them in for you. Ask them if they can double skin them for you as well.
7. Season the fish – poach it off in butter for 6-7 minutes and then colour it off in a hot pan.
8. Sauté purple sprouting broccoli and samphire in a hot pan. Bring each element of the dish together on a plate and drizzle the butter from the poaching pan over the top. Done!

No4 Choc ice

Serves 10

Ingredients
- 300g Dark chocolate (53%)
- 250ml (9fl oz) double cream
- 80g (3oz) caster sugar
- 2 eggs
- 1 vanilla pod
- 2 tbsp Horlicks

Salt caramel
- 300g (10½oz) caster sugar
- 1 tbsp water
- 150g (5½oz) unsalted butter
- 200ml (7oz) double cream
- Crushed roasted peanuts (to serve)
- Clotted cream (to serve)

1. Melt the dark chocolate in a bowl and line 10 silicone moulds with the liquid chocolate – set in the fridge.
2. For the semifreddo, split 2 eggs then whisk the yolks and caster sugar in a food processor. Whisk the whites until in stiff peaks. Fold the fluffy whites into the yolk and sugar mix and whisk in the mixer. Whisk double cream and Horlicks powder together. Fold into the egg mixture.
3. Put the mixture into a piping bag and pipe it into the set chocolate cases – pop in the freeze to set. Once set cover the tops with more chocolate and pop back in the freezer.
4. Crush peanuts and add salt caramel – lush!

NOLA'S TIPS FOR HOLDING YOUR OWN FEAST NIGHT

FEAST NIGHTS CAN BE A FUN WAY OF BRINGING ALL SORTS OF DIFFERENT PEOPLE TOGETHER OVER GOOD FOOD.

• It sounds basic, but the key thing is to make sure you've got enough bowls, plates and cutlery.
• Make sure everyone has somewhere to sit and mix people up a bit, so they break out of their usual groups and meet new people.

Keep the menu simple:

• For starters plate-up share platters ready to hand around.
• For mains make a slow-cooked pot of something that you can serve banquet-style.
• Then serve an easy dessert – nothing that can go wrong, or requires much preparation on the night.
• Always serve a cheese board.
• Have a great selection of wine and it will be fine.

CORNISH ARTISAN BEER

{REBEL BREWING COMPANY}

No.4 serves artisan beers handcrafted by the Rebel Brewing Company in Penryn. Cornwall's coolest and most dynamic microbrewery, Rebel is passionate about making unique, high-quality craft beers in the most sustainable way possible.

Striving to push the boundaries of flavour, Rebel produce a core range of classic ales – from golden ale to dark scotch ale – as well as a specialist range, including a chocolate vanilla stout made using cocoa from Chocolarder artisan chocolate makers in Penryn. Previously a mining engineer, Head brewer Rob Lowe turned his hand to brewing in 2011, and as well as selling his beers to some of the best foodie haunts in Cornwall, he already supplies Rebel beers to bars and restaurants nationally.

These are our top 3 Rebel Brewery beers to sink by the beach in Cornwall:

Surfbum IPA

This 3.5% Californian-style IPA uses distinctive hops from some of the best surfing countries around the globe to make a light hoppy beer. Perfect after an awesome summer surf in the Cornish sunshine.

Black Rock Bitter

Named after the legendary Black Rock that sits in the mouth of Falmouth Harbour, this is the perfect autumn tipple when you've sailed into harbour and moored up for the evening. A velvety copper ale with a nutty, biscuit flavour and the scent of smoked woodchip on the nose, it also goes wonderfully with a hearty harvest feast.

Cornish Sunset

Named after the Cornish sunset, this golden ale is strong and golden when going down, with a lasting bitterness when it's gone. Crisp and refreshing, it's zesty on the nose with a clean finish, making it an ideal accompaniment to spicy foods.

Sunday Lunch
Live Music —

♥ Saturday 14th Fe
Live Music from
♥ 'Jumping Out Dr
Special Valentine
dinner being so
♥ (please see mon
February
1st - Zena + the Jaz
Warriors
8th - Funny Feathe
15th - First + Last
22nd - Bar Fly.
March
1st - Liam Jordan
8th - Funny Feathe
15th - The Cuts
22nd - BT Experie
29th - Kaj.

FEEL THE BEAT

Love music and love food? Here's our pick of beachside bars where you can listen to some cool tunes, grab a decent bite to eat and sink a pint while the sun goes down.

■ BLUE BAR, PORTHTOWAN

Serving up live music, comedy nights and cracking sunsets alongside cocktails and legendary Blue Burgers, this beach bar has been one of the county's coolest venues to eat, drink, dance and chill out surfside for over a decade. Bask on the terrace or gaze out to the Atlantic rollers from behind big bay windows while you feast on hearty fare and tune into internationally-acclaimed artists playing in a world-class setting.
www.blue-bar.co.uk

■ THE PHOENIX, WATERGATE BAY

Footsteps from the watersports Mecca of Watergate Bay, The Phoenix is a cracking spot to catch live bands, sip a sundowner and fuel up on sumptuous surfside grub. The combination of easy access to the surf, a cosy and contemporary inside, and a wide sea-view decking make this a popular haunt year-round.
www.phoenixwatergate.co.uk/the-phoenix

■ THE WATERING HOLE, PERRANPORTH

Bang on Perranporth's two-mile beach this is one of Cornwall's coolest beach bars, with a year-round line-up of live music from surfy singer-songwriters to top British bands and world-class DJs. The food and drink is crowd-pleasing and unpretentious – stacks of nachos and fat burgers perfect for fuelling up after a surf. If you bag a bench surfside, make sure the seagulls don't steal your chips while you're tuned into the music with your eyes fixed on a cracking sunset.
www.thewateringhole.co.uk

■ GYLLY BEACH CAFÉ, FALMOUTH

Flaunting a cool and contemporary vibe from its beachside vantage point, this is Falmouth's hottest hangout for food, wine and some fancy footwork on the dancefloor. Lounge on the terrace with cocktails and canapés, come inside for a candle-lit dinner conjured from fresh local ingredients, or catch one of the crowd-pulling music nights with tunes spilling out from the bar to the beach.
www.gyllybeach.com

■ SAND BAR, PRAA SANDS

True to its name, a trail of sand follows punters from the beach into this trendy bar overlooking one of the south coast's most popular surf breaks. The Mediterranean-influenced menu would lure plenty of custom regardless of the panoramic sea views, but to add to the venue's pulling points there's a seriously good schedule of live music, including bands accompanying the Sunday carvery.
www.sandbarpraasands.co.uk

DOWN BY THE RIVER

SECRET RETREATS, OYSTER FARMS, AND TREE-FRINGED CREEKS

RE-WILDING, FURRY UNDERGROUND CHICKENS AND WILD FOOD

Meandering through an Area of Outstanding Natural Beauty stretching from Truro to Falmouth, the Fal River is an ancient flooded valley hemmed by native woodland. Its network of waterways is popular with sailors who explore its tidal tributaries and drop anchor at beauty spots such as Trelissick Garden at Feock and the Pandora Inn at Restronguet.

One of Cornwall's most popular visitor destinations, there's plenty to lure people to the river and its surroundings, from castles and beaches to walking trails and sub-tropical gardens. FROM THE WOODS TO THE WATER, THE ENTIRE AREA IS TEEMING WITH WILDLIFE AND WILD INGREDIENTS. Edible seaweeds and herbs line its shores, and one of the world's only traditional oyster fishing fleets still dredge the river under sail and oar.

The historic King Harry chain ferry crosses the river at Philleigh, linking the outskirts of Truro to the remote beauty of the Roseland Peninsula. Making the most of the natural environment and the abundance of wild ingredients that thrive here, 7th Rise offers fishing, foraging, hunting and wild food cookery experiences in a secret woodland location on the Roseland side of the river.

IT'S A WILD, WILD, LIFE!

{7TH RISE}

Keen to share his enthusiasm for bush craft, hunting and wild food, Thom Hunt runs foraging, hunting and wild cookery experiences in the woods by the River Fal. Whisking participants out of civilisation and into a wild and remote location, his base is a once derelict cottage hidden in ancient oak woodland, a 15-minute walk from the nearest lane. The water supply is diverted from the stream and, aside from the stone cottage, the entire site – fireside seating, a creek-side bar, an outdoor kitchen and treehouse accommodation – has been crafted from local, sustainable wood. But it's not completely uncivilised – there are flushing toilets and at the bar you can order a range of nature's tipples including elderflower champagne and nettle beer.

From bow and arrow fishing to cooking on the open fire, food is integral to 7th Rise adventures. "There's a groundswell in people wanting to know where their food comes from," Thom explains. "Here you will learn where it lived, how to catch it, and how to prepare and cook it." Chef extraordinaire, Matt Vernon, used to freedive for mussels on the Fal River and is a keen forager with a flair for cooking with wild ingredients. "Cooking has always been my passion, but I'm not into the high-pressure environment of cheffing. I love playing around with wild ingredients," he says. "I grew up foraging and cooking.

WE TURNED OUR GARDEN OVER TO VEG, AND HAD A GUN TO SHOOT PHEASANT WITH. Even if I wasn't working here I'd be out picking samphire and sea beet, or foraging for mushrooms."

From fish to pheasant, the ingredients Matt uses are almost all wild, sustainable and local. "Food is real here. We can trace all of the food we use back to its roots. The only time we

go to the supermarket is for things like coffee." One of Matt's favourite ingredients is rabbit – or 'furry underground chickens'. "It's lean, healthy, inexpensive, truly free range, and abundant," he says. "This invasive species causes around £260 million of crop damage a year and is a tasty source of protein that hasn't been intensively farmed. Eating wild rabbit is a satisfying way of helping your local farmers and your local environment." Thom shoots his own rabbits and will teach you how to butcher and prepare them for recipes such as Matt's confit rabbit leg and smoked rabbit loin.

Being by the river, catching and cooking fish is also high on the menu of foodie adventures. "We catch mackerel in the creek in summer, and fillet them immediately for sashimi or fry them up on a gas cooker by the river," says Thom – "you can't get fresher than that." Foraging along the foreshore, you never quite know what ingredients you're going to net for your next meal; it could be crabs, prawns, mussels, winkles or edible seaweeds. "When you can look at the river where you caught your ingredients, it creates a deeper sense of experience of eating the

dish," explains project co-ordinator Alice Manhire.

"WE'RE NOT RUNNING SOME SORT OF BEAR GRYLLS SURVIVAL COURSE, WE'RE SIMPLY USING SKILLS THAT HAVE BEEN AROUND FOR CENTURIES AND BRINGING PEOPLE CLOSER TO NATURE THROUGH FOOD," explains Alice. And while food is pivotal to 7th Rise courses, the experience is also about getting back to nature, going on a digital detox and having time to experience a more adventurous way of life while you enjoy activities such as swimming in the river and walking in the woods. Thom refers to the experience as 're-wilding': "Re-wilding isn't only the return of habitats to their natural state, here it's also about taking institutionalised and habitualised humans into the wild and taking them back to traditional skills and a more basic lifestyle," he explains.

FURRY UNDERGROUND CHICKENS

'Furry underground chickens' is the name given to rabbits by Cornish fishermen. They are considered bad luck to the point they won't even utter the word 'rabbit'.

However, this sustainable, abundant meat is tender, succulent, lean and tasty. It's also inexpensive and truly free range. The following methods are great ways of complementing rabbit. Don't be put off by the terms 'confit' and 'hot smoking', these are simple methods to replicate at home.

Confit Rabbit Legs
with buttered sea greens and peppered blackberry sauce

Tender and succulent with a sweet and tangy pepper sauce. Great served on buttery mashed potato. Both the confit and sauce can be made in advance.

Ingredients
Rabbit:
- 8 large rabbit legs
- 1kg dripping
- 4 fresh bay leaves
- 2 tsp peppercorns
- 6 cloves garlic

Sauce:
- 200g (7oz) blackberries
- 55g (2oz) elderberries
- 200ml (7fl oz) red wine
- Butter
- Freshly ground black pepper
- Cornish sea salt

Sea Greens:
- 340g (12oz) Sea beet
- ½ nutmeg, freshly grated

Method
Rabbit:
1. Warm oven to 130C.
2. Using a casserole dish, on a low heat melt enough lard to cover the rabbit legs. You don't want the fat to be bubbling, just a slow melt. Carefully place the legs in. It's really important to make sure the meat is covered otherwise it will dry out. If they aren't covered add more diced lard.
3. Pop in the bay leaves, peppercorns and whole garlic cloves. Cover and transfer to the oven. Cook for 3-4 hours until the meat is tender and nearly (but not quite) falling off the bone.
4. Leave to cool for safe handling. If you want to store for a few days transfer to the fridge where the fat will solidify and preserve. To remove the meat gently scrape away the fat with a spoon and tease the legs out, trying to keep the meat on the bone. Scrape away most of the dripping, leaving a small amount for frying.
6. Using a frying pan sear on a high heat to caramelise the outside of the meat. Cook until golden brown and heated through.

Sauce:
1. Melt a large knob of butter on a medium heat in a small pan.
2. Add the wine and bring to a simmer.
3. Add blackberries and crush with the back of a spoon. Add elderberries without crushing.
4. Season with salt and go nuts with the black pepper!
5. Simmer for 5 minutes on a low to medium heat.
6. Just before serving stir in another knob of butter to give the sauce extra sheen.

Sea Greens:
1. Remove any thick stalks from the sea beet.
2. Melt a knob of butter with a little oil in a pan on a medium heat.
3. Add the sea beet, nutmeg and stir.
4. Sauté for about 3-4 minutes until wilted but still with a little crunch. Stir frequently. No need to season as the sea beet is salty enough.

To serve, place the rabbit on mash potato, greens by the side, and drizzle the sauce over the legs.

ALTERNATIVE INGREDIENTS

The wild ingredients Matt uses in his cooking are not unusual or difficult to find, however it's advisable to do some research or go on a course before picking your own wild ingredients. In the meantime he suggests a few alternatives you can buy to replace the wild ingredients in his recipes:

Mustard leaves: wholegrain mustard and horseradish
Hogweed seeds: loose leaf tea and coriander seeds
Rock samphire: coriander leaves and grated carrot
Common sorrel: lemon zest
Sea beet: Swiss chard
Mushroom ketchup: soy sauce

Hogweed Smoked Rabbit Loin on Samphire Cakes with Wild Mustard Dressing

Fragrant rabbit with zesty samphire and sorrel, and a subtle mustard heat.

Ingredients

Serves 4 (as a starter)

Rabbit:
- 8 loins wild rabbit
- 4 tbsp hogweed seeds

Samphire cakes:
- 600g (2oz) potatoes
- 40g (1½oz) rock samphire, coarsely chopped
- 30g (1oz) butter
- ½ lemon, zest only

Warm dressing:
- 60ml (2fl oz) crème fraîche
- 30ml (1fl oz) West Country cider
- 5g (17oz) mustard leaves, coarsely chopped
- Freshly ground black pepper
- Cornish sea salt

Garnish:
- 1 tsp common sorrel, finely chopped

Method

Samphire Cakes:
1. Boil potatoes, drain and mash with the butter.
2. Stir in the rock samphire and lemon zest thoroughly. Season to taste.
3. Spread the potato mix out on a large plate so it cools quickly. When it has cooled transfer to the fridge for at least an hour, this will help the mix to firm up. Even better refrigerate overnight.
4. Form into small round cakes, about 2 per person.
5. Fry on a medium heat in a little oil until golden and crispy on the outside.

Rabbit:
1. To smoke the loins you will need a heavy based pan with a steamer or metal sieve. Line the bottom of the pan with several layers of tin foil and evenly spread the hogweed seeds over the foil. Place the loins in the steamer or sieve and put in the pan, then cover and seal with tin foil.
2. Put the pan on a medium heat and when the seeds start to smoke turn down low. The loins will take about 10 minutes to cook depending on the size.
3. Make a small incision to check the meat is cooked through. Remove as soon as they are done, as overcooking will dry the meat.

Warm dressing:
1. When the loins are nearly done start putting together the dressing.
2. Pour the cider into a small pan on a medium heat and bring to a simmer.
3. Turn the heat down low and stir in the crème fraîche. Don't simmer or boil the sauce, gently warm and stir.
4. Remove from the heat and stir in the chopped mustard leaves. Don't return to the heat as the mustard will lose its flavour.
5. Plate up the cakes, arrange the loins on top, and drizzle sauce over. Garnish with the sorrel.

Pulled Venison in Big Vern's Smoky Sauce

Melt-in-the-mouth venison with a soul-warming sauce.

Ingredients

Serves 6 - 8

Sauce:

- 2 medium red onions, sliced
- 2 red or yellow peppers, sliced
- 800g (1lb 12oz) passata
- 4 tsp smoked paprika
- 4 tsp allspice
- 2 tsp tamarind paste
- 1 lemon, zest and juice
- 2 tsp sugar
- Butter
- Cooking oil

Venison:

- 1kg (2lbs 3oz) whole venison haunch
- 4 bay leaves
- 4 sprigs of rosemary

Method

Venison:

1. In a very hot frying pan with a little oil, brown the meat all over.
2. Place the venison on a steaming rack over the herbs in a large lidded casserole dish. Add water, making sure the meat isn't in contact with it.
3. Cover and cook on a low heat for 3-4 hours until the meat is falling apart. Keep checking every 20-30 minutes and top up with more hot water when needed.
4. When the meat is so tender that it is falling apart, place it on a large board then pull apart into shreds using a fork.

Sauce (this tastes even better if you make it the day before):

1. Cut the onion in half and slice into long thin strands, this gives great texture to the finished sauce.
2. Cook the onions and peppers on a low to medium heat in butter and oil for at least 20 minutes, or until the onions are nice and gooey.
3. Add spices, lemon zest, sugar and tamarind. Stir to coat onions and peppers.
4. Add lemon juice to de-glaze the pan.
5. Add passata and bring to a slow simmer. Cover and cook for approximately 45 minutes.
6. When the sauce is ready stir in the shredded venison, taste and season.

Serve in a wrap or crusty bun with freshly sliced onion, tomato, and salad leaves.

KEEP IT WILD!

Wild Satay Venison Skewers

Creamy and sweet chestnut. Great cooked on the BBQ.

Ingredients

Makes around 10-12 skewers

Venison:
- 500g (1lb 2oz) venison rump, roughly 2cm cubed

Sauce:
- 1 medium red onion, diced
- 400ml (14fl oz) coconut milk
- 200g (7oz) chestnuts, roasted, peeled, roughly chopped
- Thumb-sized piece of ginger, freshly grated
- 1 lemon, zest and juice
- 4 tsp ras-el-hanout spice mix
- 3 tsp mushroom ketchup
- Butter
- Oil
- Cornish sea salt

Method

Sauce:

1. Get the onions cooking before any other prep. Sauté the onions in butter and oil on a low to medium heat for at least 20 minutes so that they are soft and gooey.
2. Once the onions are ready stir in the ras-el-Hanout, ginger, mushroom ketchup, and lemon zest and juice to create a paste. Sauté for a few minutes to infuse.
3. Add the chestnuts and coconut milk and stir. Turn up the heat to medium and simmer for 20 minutes.
4. Once the sauce has thickened season to taste if needed.

Venison:

1. Keep back some sauce for later.
2. Coat the diced venison in the sauce and skewer. If you can, prepare in advance to give the meat a chance to marinate.
3. You can pan fry this but in my opinion it really is best cooked over hot coals or an open fire. The smoke adds another dimension.
4. For medium rare, BBQ over a hot heat, turning regularly until the sauce starts to slightly char all over.

Serve with the remainder of the sauce warmed and ready for dipping.

EAT FROM THE SHORELINE

Plucking most of his food from the shoreline around the Fal River, Matt Vernon talks us through some of his favourite shoreline edibles:

Sea beet

These glossy, succulent leaves (like superior spinach) are very versatile and a great replacement for leafy greens in common family recipes. For example, I like to replace the spinach in Sag Aloo with sea beet. I also use them in salads and blanch them to serve alongside meat and fish dishes.

Hogweed

The leaves have a sharp, peppery, almost pickled flavour. One of my favourite uses for them is to make tempura hogweed shoots served with rabbit. The seeds are very aromatic too, so I use these in rice dishes.

Spear-leaved orache

A versatile wild herb that is able to tolerate the salinity of the riverbanks, spear-leaved orache is abundant around the Fal throughout the summer. The young tender leaves are great in salads – sweet and nutty with a hint of salt.

Scurvy Grass

Packs a bitter horseradish punch into a tiny leaf. As a garnish it adds little bullets of intense flavour to a dish.

Salty Fingers

These look like jelly beans but they pop in your mouth with a salty burst. Adds fun to any salad or as a garnish for seafood.

Wild mustard flowers

Again abundant in areas rich in salinity, I love adding these to salads to give them a strong, peppery boot.

Sea Campion flowers

Beautiful pale petals with tones of pink and purple that will add a splash of colour to the plate with hints of mild, sweet aniseed.

Common sorrel

A very common ingredient in the damp woodland around the river, common sorrel has a lovely lemony hint to it, so is perfect to chop up and sprinkle over a variety of dishes.

TIPS FOR CATCHING AND GUTTING YOUR OWN FISH

IN AND AROUND FALMOUTH THERE ARE SOME GREAT COASTAL FISHING SPOTS – FROM THE UPPER REACHES OF THE RIVER FAL, AROUND TO PENDENNIS POINT, AND ONWARDS TO STACK POINT OFF SWANPOOL BEACH. MACKEREL, BASS, WRASSE AND BREAM ARE COMMON IN THESE WATERS.

A successful fishing trip is part luck, part preparation, all patience, and lots of fun. Maybe you will catch dinner or maybe you will just enjoy the quiet contemplation of a beautiful view.

1. KNOW YOUR GROUND. If you are going to a particular spot, find out which species will feed in this habitat. For example, is it a sandy or rocky bottom?

2. KNOW YOUR TARGET. Make sure you have the right bait and equipment for the species you want to catch. Is it the right time of year? What does the species prefer to feed on?

3. PREPARE. Make sure you have all the equipment you need and get to your spot at the right tide or time. Check the tides and weather before you set out.

RENAISSANCE BEACH TOWN

TALL SHIPS, TALLER TALES, GOOD VIBES AND PUFFED WHITE SAILS

EXPLODING FOODIE SCENE AND A
TOWN STEEPED IN MARITIME HERITAGE

Not only a town of maritime heritage, sandy beaches, bucketfuls of history and a buzzing art and music scene, Falmouth is now undergoing something of a foodie resurgence, too.

Sitting at the entrance to the world's third deepest harbour, it was during the 17th century that Falmouth was transformed from a fishing village into one of the most important packet ship ports in the UK. A booming maritime scene ensued, and to this day sailing, fishing and shipbuilding are still linchpins of the town's economy.

Also home to one of the UK's leading art and media universities, the sails have been hoisted on Falmouth's creative scene, with art galleries, literary gatherings, a ripple of cultural events and a thriving live music scene. Add to that a cluster of sandy beaches linked by stunning coastal walks, and you'll find there's plenty to do here both on land and on the water.

Framed by the ocean and an Area of Outstanding Natural Beauty, it's little surprise that FALMOUTH IS BECOMING WELL KNOWN FOR THE WEALTH OF EXCELLENT PRODUCE PLUCKED FROM ITS SURROUNDINGS. All manner of local ingredients, from shellfish to locally roasted coffee, is served up in the smattering of cool cafés and fine dining restaurants that grace the town and its beaches.

POSITIVE ENERGY & SUPERFOOD

{GOOD VIBES}

John and Hannah Hersey, the owners of Good Vibes Café, are passionate about the provenance of their ingredients, while also creating the sort of dishes that stoke people's energy for the beach lifestyle on their doorstep.

"It's the nutrition and freshness of our food that's inspired by the coast more than the actual ingredients," John explains. "We're really into our fitness, and so are a lot of our customers. There's a huge watersports community here in Falmouth – paddle boarders, sailors, kayakers, swimmers and surfers. So a lot of our inspiration comes from providing really wholesome, energising food." No strangers to the active coastal lifestyle in question, John and Hannah are driven by their love of the sea and spend as much time as possible surfing.

"LIKE LOTS OF PEOPLE AROUND HERE, WE LIVE HEALTHILY AND DO A LOT OF ACTIVITY, AND OUR MENU IS GEARED TOWARDS THAT," they explain. It was when they were travelling in Spain and Portugal that John and Hannah set their hearts on starting up a café. "We were inspired by the couple that set up Shells Café in the Surf Café Cookbook," Hannah explained. "We love food and living by the sea, and decided we wanted to make a living out of it." With the interior of Good Vibes bedecked in up-cycled furniture, cool surf prints and worktops that still resemble the tree trunks they were carved from, they have succeeded in following their dream and recreating a cool coastal vibe resonant of their travels.

Although Falmouth is well endowed with eateries, Good Vibes stands out for its provision of fairly priced breakfasts and lunches using exceptional ingredients. "We're lucky that there are so many really good suppliers down here, so we can source a lot of our staples within Cornwall," says John. "We aim to serve the sort of food you can eat every day, at the sort of price it would cost to go out and buy the ingredients."

Top of the bill is a range of legendary sandwiches, from crumbled blue cheese, beetroot, pumpkin and orange chutney, to the signature sweet cure Cornish bacon with guacamole, hummus and smoked paprika. Then there is fresh soup and crunchy salads that change with the seasons. The couple make all their own cakes – including their famous raspberry mocha brownies – while Da Bara Bakery create bespoke bread and pastries for the café. Rating good coffee as highly as good food, John also reckons they've managed to source "pretty much the best coffee on earth" from Cornish coffee roasters Yallah and Origin.

"People have positive energy and give off good vibes when they eat well," explains Hannah, "and that's really where our name came from." On the wall hangs a blackboard inscribed with a little ditty: 'Live in the sunshine, Swim in the sea, Drink delicious coffee & tea.' Sandwiches stuffed with superfoods only cost a fiver. The clientele swap stories of their beach adventures. This is evidently the sort of café where the 'Good Vibes' are most definitely flowing.

SANDWICHES

ADD A CUP OF SOUP FOR £1.50

SMOKED STREAKY BACON, OLE & SMOKED PAPRIKA. TAKEOUT: £4.50

ITH FREE RANGE EGG, FRON MAYO, CUCUMBER N: £5 • TAKEOUT: £4.50

TED CHICKEN WITH & CHILI RELISH AND KY PESTO. TAKEOUT: £4.50

KERNOW SAUSAGE WITH SMOKED TINTAGEL CHEDDAR, ONION & TOMATO CHUTNEY AND STICKY BBQ SAUCE. EAT IN: £5 • TAKEOUT: £4.50

CRUMBLED BLUE CHEESE WITH BEETROOT, PUMPKIN & ORANGE CHUTNEY AND PINK ONIONS (V) EAT IN: £4.75 • TAKEOUT: £4.25

SPICED CHICKPEA & CARROT HUMMUS WITH ARTICHOKES, RE CUCUMBER (VEG) EAT IN: £4.75 • TAKEOUT: £4.25

John's Sunrise Salad

A beautiful salad, inspired by the colours and textures that are around in nature at autumn time. Very simple to make – but with the extra effort of pickling the garnishes and the freshly squeezed, zesty orange dressing – this is a real treat and packed full of vitamins and nutrients.

Ingredients
(*Serves 2*)

- 100g (4oz) mixed organic baby salad leaves
- Handful of parsley and sorrel
- 3 ripe figs
- 75g (2½oz) pecan nuts
- 150g (5oz) soft goat's cheese
- ¼ red onion
- ½ small cucumber
- 2 radishes
- 3 tbsp cider vinegar
- 1 orange, zest and juice
- 25ml (1fl oz) pure maple syrup
- 1 tsp balsamic vinegar
- 2 tsp extra virgin olive oil
- Salt and pepper

Method

1. Finely slice the red onion, cucumber and radishes, pop in a bowl and add the cider vinegar. Make sure everything has a good vinegary coat, add a small amount of the parsley and leave aside to pickle whilst preparing the rest of the salad.
2. Chop figs into quarters, and roughly chop the walnuts. Add these to a mixing bowl along with the leaves, parsley and sorrel leaves.
3. Crumble over the soft goat's cheese – the small bits will melt down with the dressing, and the larger bits will add luxurious pockets of cheesy goodness.
4. In a separate bowl whisk up the juice of the orange with the maple syrup, olive oil, balsamic vinegar, and season to taste.
5. Add to the mixing bowl with your leaves, herbs, figs and walnuts, mix through the pickles and lightly toss, drizzle in the dressing slowly until all the leaves and ingredients are coated with the sweet syrup.
6. Give it a hit of cracked black pepper and orange zest to finish the job. Tuck in.

Good Vibes Café's Signature Sandwich

Fresh, filling, healthy and delicious, this is on our menu every day, all year round. It's smoky, creamy, crunchy and wholesome, and uses healthy super foods – avocados and chickpeas.

(Serves 2)

Ingredients

- 2 long soft ciabatta loaves
- 100g (4oz) crisp organic salad leaves
- Spanish sweet smoked paprika (the best you can get your hands on)
- 16 rashers smoked streaky bacon

Guacamole:

- 3 large ripe avocados,
- 1 large ripe vine tomato
- Handful parsley
- Handful coriander
- ½ lemon, zest and juice
- ½ lime, zest and juice
- ½ red onion, chopped finely
- 1 clove garlic

Hummus:

- 1 tin chickpeas
- ½ lemon, zest
- 1 clove garlic
- Splash cider vinegar
- 1 tsp cumin
- 1 tsp turmeric
- 1 tsp coarse sea salt
- 1 tbsp tahini
- ½ tsp cracked black pepper

Method

For the hummus:

1. Put all the ingredients in a heavy bottomed saucepan and heat and stir slowly, coating the chickpeas with the spices and seasoning.
2. Add a few splashes of water, take off the heat and blend with a hand blender, or put in a food mixer and blitz to a smooth consistency.

For the guacamole:

1. Peel, stone and slice the avocados. Crush and chop the fresh garlic, finely dice the red onion and chop the herbs.
2. Add to a mixing bowl with the rest of the ingredients and mash with a big wooden spoon or, if you like, use your hands and get messy. Season with some extra black pepper and chilli flakes (optional) for an extra kick.

Assembling the sandwich:

1. Grill the bacon so its crispy, adding some smoked paprika half way through. This makes the kitchen smell even better and gives a bigger kick!
2. Grill or toast the ciabatta, smear each side with the delicious fresh guacamole and hummus, add the leaves and finally the bacon, and then just throw smoked paprika all over the place! The smooth fragrant hummus and fresh, creamy, herby guacamole can handle the dry smokiness and the bacon juices will ooze through.
3. Squeeze down, shove in your mouth and feel epic!

Slow Burner Dry Rub Chicken with a Tarragon and Cashew Slaw

This is absolutely fantastic to cook and share with friends on a summer evening, sat outside with a few beers. The dish is fragrant, earthy, smoky, herby and exciting, and relies on nothing more than a great quality free-range chicken and some patience. The custom dry rub is easy to knock up in a few minutes and adds so much flavour. If you fancy serve it up with fresh watercress or sorrel and grill up some sourdough to mop up the juices.

Ingredients
- Whole roast chicken (about 2.5kg)
- 2 lemons

Dry Rub:
- 1 tsp cumin seeds
- 1 star anise
- 1 tsp fennel seeds
- 1 tsp mustard seeds
- 1 cinnamon stick
- 2 cardamom pods
- 2 cloves
- 4 black peppercorns
- Small chunk of nutmeg
- Sprig fresh rosemary
- Sprig fresh thyme
- 2 tsp paprika (smoked)
- 2 tsp cayenne pepper

Slaw:
- ½ sweetheart cabbage
- ½ red cabbage
- 1 large carrot
- 40g (1½oz) chopped fresh tarragon
- 75g (2½oz) chopped cashew nuts
- Handful parsley, chives and coriander
- 300g jar of good mayonnaise
- Cracked black pepper

Method
1. Preheat oven to 140C. 'Spatchcock' the chicken by turning it breast side down with feet towards you, use some culinary scissors to cut either side of the 'parsons nose' and remove the backbone and giblets inside the chicken. Turn back over and deeply score the chicken through the skin, right into the flesh, giving big juicy crevices for the dry rub to find its way into.
2. In a heavy bottom pan, slowly heat and toast the cumin seeds, star anise, fennel seeds, cinnamon stick, cardamom pods, cloves, mustard seeds, peppercorns and nutmeg. Once they start to become lively and fragrant in the pan, transfer into a pestle and mortar along with the paprika and cayenne pepper and grind into a powder – the smell at this point will give you an idea of the way this recipe is going.
3. Drizzle some olive oil over the prepared chicken and work your spice rub all over it, covering every last bit and using all of the dry rub mix. Once seasoned, put in a roasting tin on top of the quartered lemons and cook for 2 hours at 140C, (or longer depending on the size of the chicken). Once cooked through, rest under tin foil for 15 minutes before serving – this will ensure the chicken pulls effortlessly off the bones.

For the Slaw:
1. No fancy equipment needed. With a sharp knife, finely slice the sweetheart and red cabbage, and coarsely grate the carrot. Roughly chop all of the herbs (tarragon, parsley, chives and coriander) and, in a big bowl, mix in the whole jar of mayonnaise and the cashews, then squeeze lemon juice and season to taste with black pepper.

Serve on a big plank of wood with some fresh watercress and toast for the ultimate sharing platter.

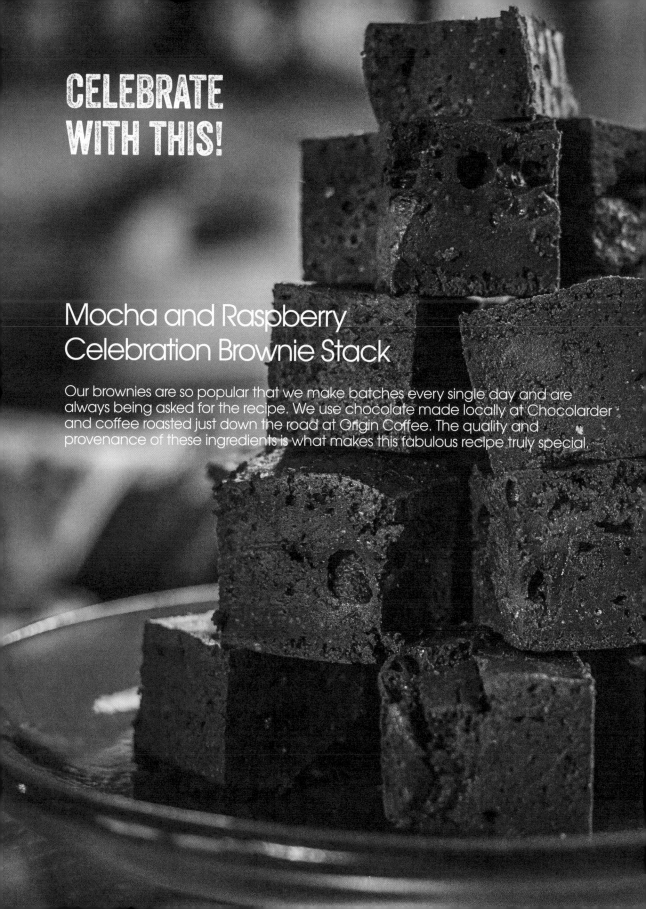

CELEBRATE WITH THIS!

Mocha and Raspberry Celebration Brownie Stack

Our brownies are so popular that we make batches every single day and are always being asked for the recipe. We use chocolate made locally at Chocolarder and coffee roasted just down the road at Origin Coffee. The quality and provenance of these ingredients is what makes this fabulous recipe truly special.

(Serves 2)

Ingredients

For the Brownies:
- 300g (11oz) 80% Dominican Republic dark chocolate from Chocolarder
- 170g (6oz) strongly brewed Origin seasonal filter coffee or espresso
- 150g (5oz) raspberries
- 400g (14oz) soft dark brown sugar (unrefined)
- 250g (9oz) salted butter
- 5 large free-range eggs
- 50g (2oz) 100% cocoa powder
- 160g (5½oz) plain flour

For the garnish:
- Small handful blueberries
- Small handful raspberries
- Sliced figs
- Handful grated white chocolate

Method

1. Preheat oven to 180C. In a heavy bottomed large pan, melt down the butter on a low heat. Whilst it's melting, add the chopped chocolate, with the soft dark sugar, and coffee. Slowly and patiently over the low heat, stir into a smooth melted batter.

2. Take off the heat and let cool slightly, before adding and stirring in the eggs one by one, making sure the last is fully mixed before adding the next one. The mix will become thicker and shiny.

3. Add the cocoa powder into the pan and sieve in the flour and a pinch of salt, keep stirring slowly and firmly until a smooth mix is achieved.

4. Add the raspberries and give another firm mix to break them down slightly. Pour the mix into a 9-inch square lined tin, and bake at 180C for 40 minutes, or until the brownie just bounces back to a light press on the top.

5. Cool to room temperature then refrigerate for a couple of hours (this will help when cutting into cubes).

6. Once chilled, remove from the tray and cut into 16 bite-sized cubes, then stack into a pyramid, being as creative as you like with the garnishes.

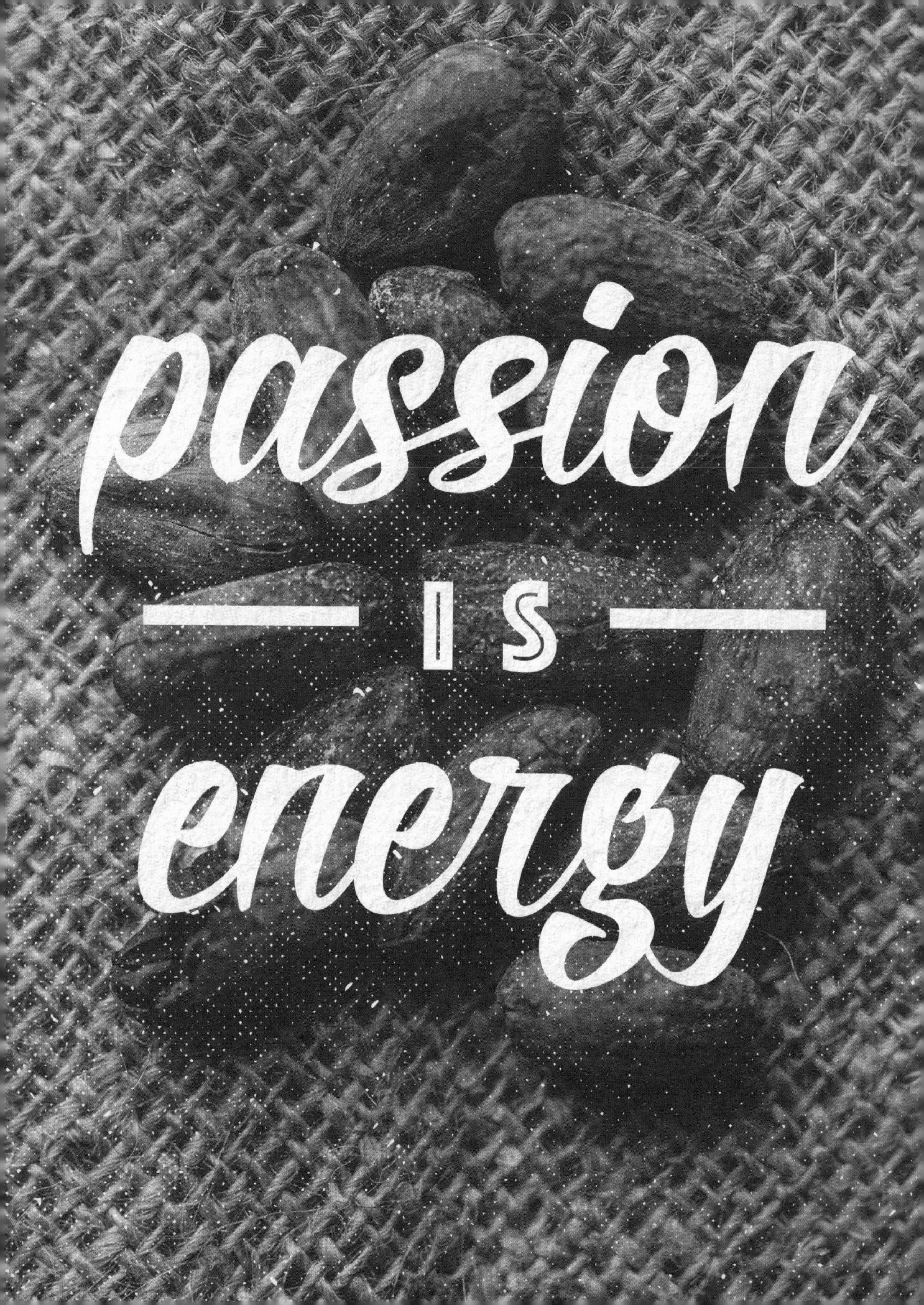
passion
is
energy

BEAN TO BAR

{HAND CRAFTED CHOCOLATE FROM CHOCOLARDER}

Emphasising their love of produce with impeccable provenance, Good Vibes make their famous brownies using only 80% Dominican Republic Dark Chocolate made by Chocolarder in Penryn. Mike Longman – Cornwall's own Willy Wonka – set up Chocolarder in 2012 and is one of just a handful of artisan chocolate makers in Britain.

He sources only the best quality raw beans from family-owned plantations in Peru, the Dominican Republic, Java and Ecuador, which undergo a process of roasting, grinding and alchemizing to produce chocolate. "The entire process, from bean to bar, is done here in Penryn," says Mike.

Having spent several years working as a pastry chef, Mike turned his hand to making chocolate because he wanted to create a product based on principles he believes should be at the heart of all good food:

"UNADULTERATED SENSORY ENJOYMENT WITHOUT COMPROMISE. NO SHORTCUTS, PRESERVATIVES, BULKING AGENTS, SUBSTITUTIONS OR ARTIFICIAL SHENANIGANS."

As well as being picky about his beans, directly sourcing them from the best growers across the globe and bringing them back to

Falmouth under sail power, Mike adds only raw cane sugar and natural Cornish flavours to create his chocolate bars.

Our favourites are the Wild Gorse Flower chocolate made from flowers picked on the Lizard Peninsula, and Cornish Honeycomb made with cold-pressed honey from bees that feed on the Lizard's wild flowers.

MAKE A GREAT CUP OF COFFEE WITH ARTISAN COFFEE MAKERS, ORIGIN.

When Tom Sobey set up Origin Coffee in 2005, his aim was to work directly with the finest coffee growers worldwide to provide traceable and sustainable coffee roasted in Cornwall. At a time when the UK's coffee culture was still in its infancy, he also wanted to deliver training and education to enable the industry to thrive. A decade later, Origin coffee – roasted in one of the world's first environmentally efficient coffee roasters – can be found in cafés throughout Cornwall and beyond, and Tom's team continues to travel the globe to source the best seasonal coffee beans from countries like Rwanda, Brazil and Ethiopia.

We asked Tom for some of his top coffee-making tips:

- Source high-quality, freshly roasted coffee.
- Grind your coffee beans no more than a minute before brewing for maximum flavour.
- Weigh the coffee to ensure optimum flavour is extracted (for filter coffee use 60-80g of freshly ground coffee per litre).
- Ensure all equipment is kept clean and rinsed free of washing-up liquid or any other flavour taints.
- Use freshly drawn water and never re-boil.
- Store coffee in a cool, dry place (but not in the fridge or freezer where the moisture will affect the coffee).
- Once brewed, leave your coffee for a few minutes before drinking to allow complex flavours to shine. Flavours will develop as the coffee cools, so resist the temptation to drink it all at once.

COFFEE
SMELLS LIKE
FRESHLY
GROUND
HEAVEN

WHERE TO GET A GREAT CUP OF COFFEE IN CORNWALL

Now that Cornwall has fully embraced the coffee culture, most towns and coastal villages have a speciality coffee shop. Here are five of our favourites where you can sip the best coffee in Cornwall:

■ RELISH, WADEBRIDGE

On a mission to serve the region's best coffee, Hugo Hercod opened the doors of Relish over a decade ago, and has since been crowned the UK's barista champion and finished in the top ten of the 'world barista' competition. Good coffee is still at the heart of this courtyard café, but it's also attracting a growing following for its delectable menu and smorgasbord of ingredients on sale in the adjoining deli.
www.relishwadebridge.co.uk

■ ESPRESSINI, FALMOUTH

This artisan coffee house in the heart of Falmouth boasts a six-foot-long menu of unique coffees from around the globe. Owner Rupert Ellis is a fully-fledged coffee connoisseur, ensuring every cup is meticulously prepared and offering a tasting wheel and notes to anyone who confesses to being part of the coffee appreciation society. However, you don't have to be a coffee-nut to enjoy the delicious brews and tasty, local food.
www.espressini.co.uk

■ THE BREW HOUSE, PORTHLEVEN

Origin's very own coffee house, The Brew House is not only a stylish harbour-side venue where exceptional Origin coffee is served, it's also headed up by Origin's most talented barista - Will Pitts. When he's not serving impeccably brewed coffee or running master classes on how to brew better coffee at home, Will is flexing his barista muscles in training for the next Barista Championships.
www.origincoffee.co.uk/the-brew-house.php

■ THE YELLOW CANARY CAFÉ, ST IVES

Set in the heart of St Ives, The Yellow Canary Café has been serving excellent coffee and pastries since 1972. As well as flawlessly brewed coffee, latte art and friendly service, this small, family-owned business offers all sorts of food from soup to homemade pasties.
www.theyellowcanary.com

■ FIG CAFÉ, TRURO

Tucked in the corner of Truro's Lemon Street Market, at Fig Café you can get your hands on excellent coffee and home-baked sweet treats - the perfect prelude to a mosey around other gems in this unique indoor market.
www.facebook.com/figcafecornwall

BISCOTTI, THE PERFECT ACCOMPANIMENT!

Fig and Almond Biscotti

These crunchy biscuits are the perfect partner to a great cup of coffee. Try this recipe from Fig Café in Truro.

Ingredients

- 110g (4oz) plain flour
- ¾ tsp baking powder
- Pinch of salt
- 4 dried figs, chopped
- 25g (1oz) ground almonds
- 50 almonds, skins on
- 75g (3oz) caster sugar
- 1 large egg, lightly beaten
- A few drops almond extract

Method

Pre-heat oven to 170C, gas mark 3

1. Sift the flour, baking powder and salt into a large bowl. Add the ground and whole almonds, sugar and figs, and give it a good mix.
2. Then add the egg and almond extract and mix together, first with a wooden spoon then using your hands to bring the mixture together to form a smooth dough.
3. Place the dough on a lightly floured surface and using your hands roll it into a log about 28cm long.
4. Put it on a lined baking sheet and bake it in the centre of the oven for 30 minutes. Transfer to a cooling tray and leave to go completely cold.
5. Reduce the oven temperature to 150C.
6. Using a serrated knife cut the biscotti into slightly diagonal slices about 1cm wide.
7. Place the pieces back on the lined baking sheet and bake for another 30 minutes until pale gold and crisp.
8. Transfer them back to the cooling tray and when cold store in an airtight container.

A
SAFE
HAVEN

WILD WAVES, HARBOUR-SIDE EATERIES AND ECHOES OF PIRACY

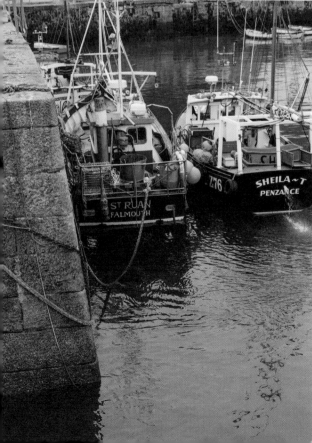

PORTHLEVEN, MOVE OVER PADSTOW

Known as 'Leven Heaven' when the surf is pumping, Porthleven is home to one of the best right-hand reef breaks in the UK. Only experienced surfers take on the hollow waves that break over a shallow rock ledge, but plenty of spectators hang out on the harbour wall to watch. When the surf is big and blown out, Porthleven's a cracking storm-watching spot too – its iconic wave-lashed clock tower becoming one of Cornwall's most photographed landmarks during the monstrous storms of 2014.

Being a harbour village that takes the brunt of the south-westerly elements, the fishermen here lose valuable trade when bad weather hits and their boats are penned in. But in more clement conditions the fishing fleet is amongst Cornwall's busiest and best, landing boatloads of fresh catch on the quay each day.

Not so long ago the town's foodie offerings stretched little further than a post-surf pasty, but now a crop of excellent restaurants plate up the day's catch alongside other Cornish-bred produce. Rick Stein has always had a nose for the next foodie destination, and it's no coincidence that he's just set up shop in Porthleven. So while walkers and naturalists are lured to Loe Bar and the Penrose Estate, and surfers hit the world-class waves, NOW FOODIES ARE FLOCKING HERE TOO; TO SAMPLE SUMPTUOUS SEAFOOD IN THE NEW WAVE OF EATERIES CLUSTERED AROUND THE PICTURESQUE HARBOUR.

SEAFOOD & STEAK

{SEADRIFT KITCHEN-CAFÉ}

Tucked away behind the harbour, SeaDrift opened its doors long before Stein sussed out Porthleven's foodie talent. Chef Chris Brooks opened his kitchen-café with his partner Carla Regler back in 2011, keeping things simple with his showcase of local seafood and Cornish steaks.

Casual by day, cosy by night, SeaDrift is an intimate venue where the menu is scrawled daily with whatever the fishermen have caught and are selling at a good price. There might be 15 different fish dishes – from oven-baked crab Florentine to simple pan-roasted hake. There is a printed menu too, comprised mostly of Cornish-reared steaks from the Lizard Peninsula that have been hung for at least 21 days.

A keen fisherman himself, Chris heads out in his own fishing boat at least once a week, and whatever he catches gets added to the menu too. "Out here you're likely to get pollock, bass, haddock, gurnard, monkfish, plaice, lemon sole and Dover sole," he says. While he gets as much of his fish as possible from Porthleven's fishing fleet, his supply can be limited in bad weather when fishing boats can't get out of the exposed harbour.

"So we get a lot of our seafood from Newlyn as well, because it's a more sheltered harbour which is always watered; and they have bigger boats so they can get out in near enough any weather," Chris explains.

Befitting of the surf scene in town, it's Chris' 'surf and turf' that's one of SeaDrift's most popular dishes. "It's the perfect post-surf meal, or ideal if you've been out boating or walking, too," he says. Although the menu is relatively simple, what's on it is homemade and hearty, down to the daily-baked bread served alongside every meal (it might be sweet chilli and cheddar, parmesan and sun-dried tomato or even carrot, horseradish and coriander). Emphasising the relaxed atmosphere, breakfast is served until two o'clock – and it's not any old breakfast, but a whopper that was recently ranked second in The Times' top 25 places for brunch in the country.

It's not only Chris' food but also his attitude that ensures the restaurant is booked up almost every evening. After service he comes out to chat to diners, and he doesn't even bother opening the restaurant if he's not there to cook. "We've got a great local following and we like to be part of the community," he says. When he's not in the kitchen or chatting to his customers he's out doing the rounds with his two dogs, stopping in at the local pubs and chatting to locals at the bar.

Pursuing Carla's passion for photography and Chris' nose for the outdoors, the couple can often be found out enjoying the coast and the lifestyle their

location encourages. Chris loves fishing and running (especially around the nearby Penrose Estate), while Carla shoots spectacular Cornish images that she sells in her gallery above the restaurant.

"WE'VE REALLY EMBRACED THE CORNISH LIFESTYLE THROUGH RUNNING THIS PLACE,"

says Chris.

Although he confesses that he hates to leave Porthleven, the pair can also be found walking the coast path from Perranuthnoe and Prussia, or between Penzance and St Ives. "We love Marazion too – it's one of Carla's favourite places to shoot," Chris says. "But I rarely leave Porthleven unless I have to. If you get out in the early morning when the sun's just up, you often see dolphins and more sea life here in 20 minutes than we did circumnavigating the Artic and Spitsbergen," he says.

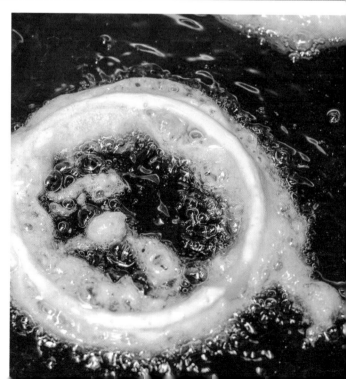

Surf 'n' Turf: Fillet Steak Topped with Seared Scallops and Tiger Prawns

Cornish steak & Cornish seafood – is there a better combination?

(Serves 1)

Ingredients

- 200/225g (6/8oz) fillet steak
- 5 tiger prawns, peeled and deveined
- 2 scallops
- 1 large vine tomato
- Olive oil
- Sea salt
- Cracked pepper
- 1 large onion, peeled
- 60g (2oz) plain flour (plus extra for dusting the onions before they go into the batter)
- 2 tsp baking powder
- 100ml (3½fl oz) water
- 125g butter, room temperature
- 1 banana shallot, finely chopped
- 2 cloves garlic, peeled and finely chopped
- Handful of mixed, fresh herbs (tarragon, parsley, coriander, chives, chervil)
- 1 lemon, cut into wedges

Batter mix

- 100g (3½oz) plain flour, sieved
- 2 tsp baking powder
- 125ml (4½fl oz) cold water

Method

1. First make the garlic butter – this needs to be done at least an hour in advance.
2. Finely chop the shallots, garlic and herbs.
3. Beat this together with the butter in a mixing bowl.
4. Spread out a thick layer of cling film, scrape the mixed garlic butter onto the cling film and roll into a sausage shape. Place into fridge to chill for use later.
5. Next make the batter for the onion rings: Sieve the flour and baking powder together into a bowl. Slowly whisk in the cold water until all the ingredients bind together.
6. Cut the onion into large rings.
7. Place tiger prawns and tomatoes (cut in half) onto a tray ready to go under the grill. Season with olive oil, salt and pepper. Add a slice of garlic butter and a wedge of lemon to the prawns.
8. Grill until cooked.
9. Season the steak with olive oil, salt, and pepper and cook to your liking in a smoking hot pan or chargrill pan. Leave it to rest while you bring the rest of the ingredients together.
10. Dust the onion rings with flour and dip into the batter mix.
11. Place into a deep fat fryer (or a pan with an inch of hot oil) at 180C and cook for 1 minute on each side until golden brown.
12. Next season the scallops with salt and pepper, put them straight onto a smoking hot pan for 20 seconds on each side, add a knob of butter and squeeze of lemon and serve straight away.
13. Place the steak back onto the grill just before plating to finish it off. Then serve the scallops, prawns, onion rings and tomatoes onto the plate. Drizzle over the garlic butter from the prawns and enjoy!

Monkfish Wrapped in Parma Ham, with Creamed Confit Cabbage and Wild Mushrooms

Monkfish is my favourite fish to eat, and I think this is the best way to enjoy it!

(Serves 1)

Ingredients

- 150g (5oz) monkfish
- 2 slices prosciutto ham
- 100g (3½oz) mixed wild mushrooms
- 2 carrots, grated
- 50ml duck fat
- 200g (7oz) savoy cabbage, shredded
- 2 cloves garlic, peeled
- 1 banana shallot
- 200ml (7fl oz) double cream
- 100ml (3½fl oz) white wine
- 1 lemon cut into wedges (1 to go into pan to cook with monkfish and 1 to serve as required)

Method

1. Shred cabbage, thinly slice shallots and garlic, and grate carrot.
2. Melt the duck fat in a pan on medium heat. Sweat off shallots and garlic for 2 minutes, add the carrot and sweat for 1 minute, add cabbage and sweat for another minute. Strain off duck fat.
3. In another hot pan, add the chopped mushrooms and sauté in olive oil and butter for about 2 minutes.
4. Season with salt and pepper. Add the white wine and drained cabbage mixture. Then add cream, bring to the boil to reduce for 5-6 minutes until it's a thick consistency.
5. Lay 2 slices of Parma ham lengthways and on a flat surface.
6. Wrap the monkfish in the ham, season with salt, pepper, olive oil.
7. Seal off the ham and monkfish in a hot pan, so all sides have been sealed in olive oil.
8. Add a knob of butter and wedge of lemon and place in the oven for 8-10 minutes at 200C (fan). Check the monkfish is cooked through.
9. Plate the cabbage (it should be a nice thick consistency) and place the monkfish wrapped in Parma ham on the top.

CHRIS'S TIPS FOR STEAK SAUCES

ALL THE STEAKS SERVED AT SEADRIFT KITCHEN-CAFÉ ARE CORNISH REARED AND AGED FOR AT LEAST 21 DAYS. IT'S THEIR PROVENANCE THAT MAKES THEM SO TENDER AND SUCCULENT, BUT IT'S ALSO CHRIS'S HOMEMADE STEAK SAUCES THAT MAKE THEM SO DELICIOUS.

His favourite steak sauces include:
- Peppercorn and brandy sauce
- Cornish Blue and red wine
- Grilled goat's cheese and basil pesto
- Wild mushroom and mustard cream sauce

Pesto and Goat's Cheese Steak Sauce

Try Chris's tips to make this tasty steak sauce.

Ingredients

- 1 shallot
- 4 cloves garlic
- 100g (3½oz) pine nuts
- 100ml (3½fl oz) extra virgin olive oil
- 12-14 basil leaves
- 50g (2oz) parmesan
- Salt and pepper to season

Method

1. Place all ingredients in a deep dish and bake in oven until the pine nuts are golden brown (180C for 35 minutes). Allow to cool.
2. Blitz ingredients in blender with the basil leaves and parmesan.
3. Cook the steak as in the other recipe, then leave to rest along with the onion rings.
4. Place the goat's cheese on top of the steak and put under the grill.
5. Drizzle pesto over the dish before serving.

Mixed Berry Pavlova

A Cornish treat… gigantic meringues, Rodda's clotted cream,
Moomaid ice cream and a few 'healthy' berries!

(Serves 6)

Ingredients

For the meringue:

- 3 egg whites
- 40g (1½oz) caster sugar
- 40g (1½oz) icing sugar
- 100ml (3½fl oz) port
- 100ml (3½fl oz) red wine
- 40g (1½oz) demerara sugar
- Handful of mixed berries, frozen or fresh

For the Chantilly Cream:

- 100ml (3½fl oz) Roddas double cream
- 100g (3½oz) Roddas clotted cream
- 50g (2oz) caster sugar
- ½ tsp vanilla essence

Method

The meringues must be made in advance.

1. Whisk egg whites until stiff. Whilst still whisking add caster sugar and whisk for a further 3-4 minutes.

2. Fold in sieved icing sugar a small amount at a time, then form into 6 even-sized quenelles (oval shaped dollops) using a serving spoon, and pop them on a baking tray lined with baking parchment.

3. Place into pre-heated oven at 100C for 1 hour 20 minutes. Turn oven off but leave them in until the oven is cold.

4. Bring the port, red wine and demerara sugar to the boil, and reduce by a third. Add mixed berries, either frozen of fresh, stir and remove from heat and chill.

5. For the Chantilly cream, whisk the double cream, clotted cream, caster sugar and vanilla until mixture becomes stiff, then refrigerate.

6. To serve, spoon over the Chantilly cream and one scoop of Moomaid vanilla ice cream. Then spoon over some berries and place one of the meringues on top. Delish!

STAY COOL!

Legend has it that once upon a time the Mermaid of Zennor lured a young Cornishman into the sea. There may no longer be mermaids in Zennor, but there is most certainly a herd of 'moomaids' – the legendary Friesian cows that help to make Moomaid of Zennor Ice Cream.

With 30 lip-smacking flavours made using milk from the dairy herd and Rodda's cream (which also uses milk from the same cows), Moomaid is one of Cornwall's favourite, and most authentic, ice cream brands. What with the Friesians grazing on coastal farmland around Zennor, and ingredients such as Cornish sea salt being used in the Sea Salt Caramel flavour, there is no other ice cream so entrenched in the Cornish coast.

Now served in restaurants, cafés and kiosks throughout the county, it's little surprise to find Moomaid being served in SeaDrift, where it goes hand in hand with the surfside setting. After all, how better to end a steak or seafood meal than with a scoop of rich, creamy Cornish ice cream?

There are all sorts of flavours from Orange and Mascarpone to Chocolate Sorbet, but Chris favours the Vanilla Bean and Clotted Cream, served with his delectable berry pavlova.

HERE ARE SOME MORE ICE CREAM TREATS SUGGESTED BY MOOMAID TO TANTALISE YOUR TASTE BUDS

Moomaid Mess:
- Vanilla ice cream
- Meringue
- Raspberry sauce
- Whole raspberries
- Pistachio nuts

Shipwreck:
- Sea salt caramel ice cream
- Dulce de leche caramel
- Cornish sea salt
- Honeycomb

Cream Tea:
- 1 scoop Cornish clotted cream ice
- 1 scoop strawberry ice cream
- Rodda's Cornish clotted cream
- Cornish strawberries

Rocky Road:
- Belgian chocolate ice cream
- Honeycomb pieces
- Malt chocolate balls
- Marshmallows

SWISH FISH RESTAURANTS

From the boat to the table – tuck into the finest
fresh fish at our top five seafood restaurants.

■ TOLCARNE INN, NEWLYN

Footsteps from Newlyn harbour, where
many of the ingredients are landed, the
Tolcarne Inn flaunts the credentials
of one of Cornwall's top seafood
restaurants while retaining the ambience
of a traditional local boozer. Helmed by
Cornish super-chef Ben Tunnicliffe, its
success has now been followed up with
another cracking seafood restaurant on
the beach at Sennen.
www.tolcarneinn.co.uk

■ HOOKED ON THE ROCKS, FALMOUTH

Overhanging Swanpool Beach, Hooked on
the Rocks hogs an enviable location. Pair
this with lashings of sumptuous Cornish
seafood – from Cornish lobster, crab and
oysters to the signature fish platter –
and there are few better places for fish
fans to bag a table.
www.hookedcornwall.com

■ BLUE PLATE, DOWNDERRY

A favourite amongst visitors and
locals alike, Blue Plate has accrued
a phenomenal reputation for its fresh,
affordable seafood. Fowey River mussels
served with Cornish cider is one of the
most popular dishes, alongside Cornish
crab and catch of the day from the Looe
fishing fleet.
www.blueplatecornwall.com

■ RESTAURANT NATHAN OUTLAW, PORT ISAAC

One of Cornwall's most eminent seafood
restaurants has relocated to Port
Isaac, where diners can gaze out to
the twinkling waters where many of the
ingredients come from. Here celebrity chef
Nathan Outlaw serves up a menu driven
by locally caught fish that's flipped
straight from local fishing boats into
delectable dishes.
www.nathan-outlaw.com

■ THE FISH HOUSE, FISTRAL

Nudging the waves on Fistral beach, The
Fish House is the sort of restaurant
that's putting Newquay bang on the foodie
map. Having grown up under the tutelage
of Rick Stein for over a decade, surfer
and chef Paul Harwood uses exquisite
ingredients in his elegant, rustic dishes
that are influenced by his surf trips
around the globe.
www.thefishhouse-fistral.com

Sustainable

Fishing

SEAFOOD AT THE BEACH

{THE FISH HOUSE}

Having worked under Rick Stein for more than a decade, Paul Harwood had always dreamed of opening his own seafood restaurant. In 2014 he achieved his vision and opened The Fish House on Fistral beach, serving up tasty local seafood at a reasonable price.

Paul's Indian Fish Curry

(Serves 4)

Ingredients

- 700g (25oz) white fish fillet (cod, pollock or hake)
- 1 small white onion
- 2 vine tomatoes
- 4 tsp dried chilli flakes
- 1 tsp cumin seeds
- 1 tsp coriander seeds
- 1 tsp salt
- 1 tsp black pepper
- 2 tsp turmeric
- 1 tsp black mustard seeds
- 90g (3oz) fresh grated coconut
- 100ml (3½oz) shellfish stock
- 40g (1oz) fresh coriander
- 5 cloves garlic
- 80ml (3floz) coconut milk
- 1 tbsp vegetable oil

Method

1. To make the masala (paste), heat the coriander seeds, cumin and black pepper in a dry pan until smoking, then transfer to a pestle and mortar and grind to a fine powder.
2. Put the onion, tomato, garlic, chilli, grated coconut and ground spices into a food processor (not including the turmeric and black mustard seeds) and blend into a paste.
3. Heat a separate wok or pan, add a tablespoon of vegetable oil and fry the turmeric and mustard seeds for 20 seconds, add the masala paste and cook on a gentle heat for 5 minutes. This paste will keep in the fridge for 3 days.
4. To make the curry put the paste, coconut milk and shellfish stock (or you can use water) into a wok and heat.
5. Gently lay your fish fillets into the sauce, cover and cook for 5 minutes.
6. Finally add your fresh coriander and check for seasoning
7. Serve with basmati rice and poppadoms.

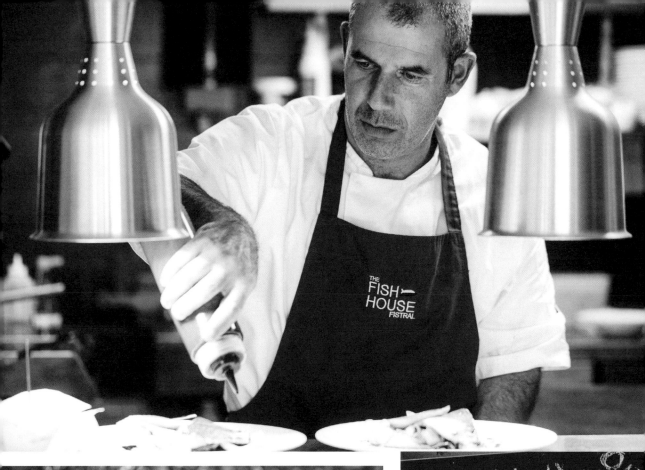

THE FISH
HOUSE
MUSSELS - £6.50
Tiger Prawns - £6.50
Fish Finger
Sandwich - £6.95
SQUID - £6.50
Seabass - £6.50
Plus lots MORE
SEAFOOD
OPEN

THE WILD LARDER

A SUB-TROPICAL LANDSCAPE PACKED WITH NATURAL INGREDIENTS

FORAGING IN ROCK POOLS AND HEDGES AT THE TIP OF CORNWALL

The coastline curling around the western toe of Cornwall is teeming with wildlife, shipwrecks and sub-tropical foliage. Follow the coast path from Marazion to Sennen and discover wild, white-sand beaches at the foot of towering granite cliffs, encounter rare sea birds such as soft-plumaged petrels and black-browed albatrosses, and clap your eyes on marine life from basking sharks to seals and dolphins.

Aside from Land's End, one of the most visited parts of this rugged hunk of coast is Porthcurno. Here the Minack Theatre stages plays in an amphitheatre at the water's edge, and Porthcurno Telegraph Museum marks what was once the epicentre of international communications when the first undersea telegraph cables were laid in 1870. However, it's Porthcurno's easy-to-reach pearly sands lapped by Caribbean-blue seas that are the real crowd puller.

While visitors flock to the area to snorkel, swim and stomp along the South West Coast Path, many of them overlook the abundance of wild ingredients that flourish from the seashore to the hedgerows. **CLIFF-TOPS ARE THRIVING WITH SAMPHIRE, GORSE FLOWERS AND WILD GARLIC, BOULDERS ARE STREWN WITH EDIBLE SEAWEEDS, AND HEDGEROWS ARE BURSTING WITH ALL SORTS OF BERRIES AND HERBS.** Take a spin to Sennen and you can top-up foraged ingredients with fresh seafood and crabs from the local fishermen.

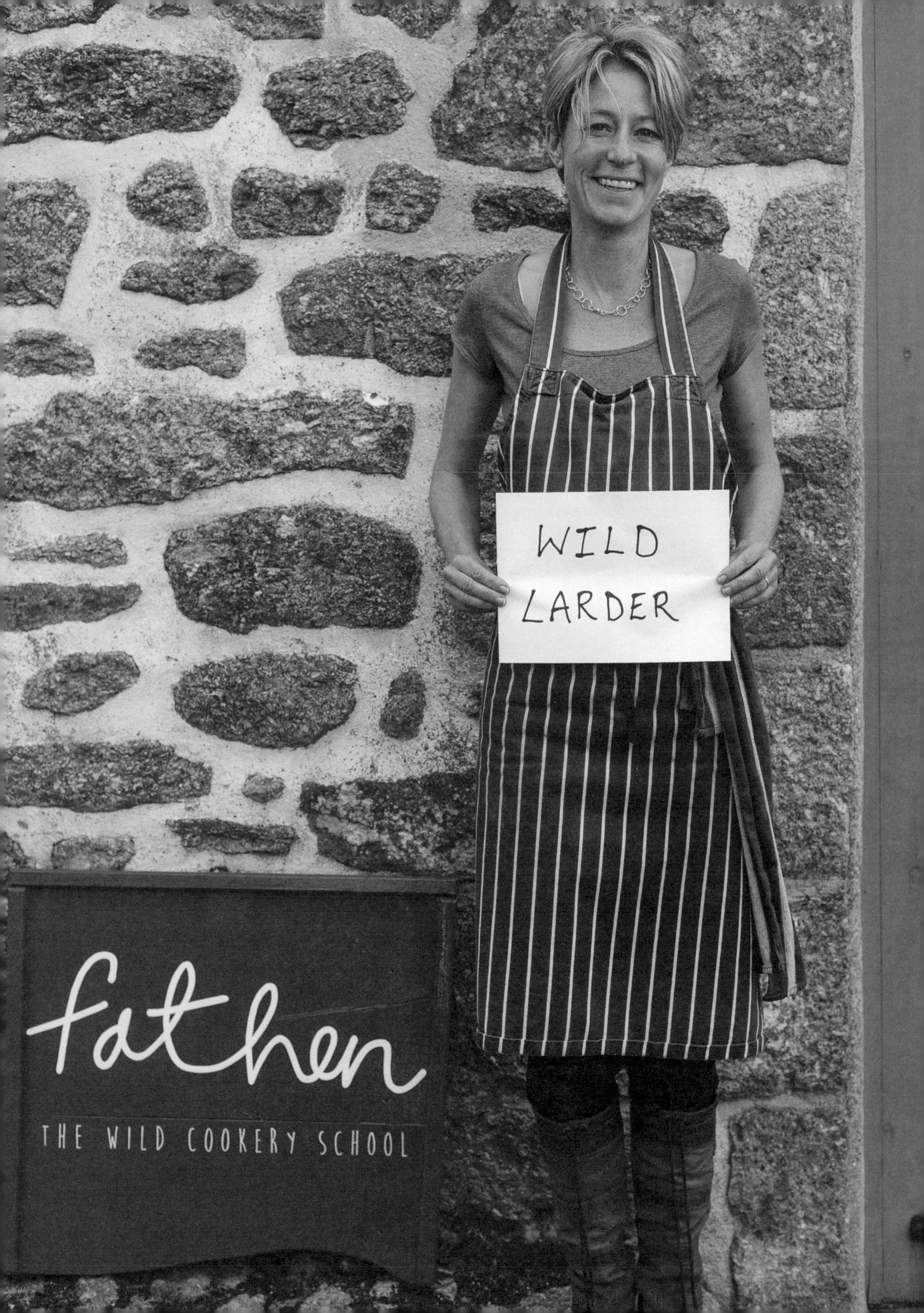
WILD
LARDER
fat hen
THE WILD COOKERY SCHOOL

SEASONAL TREASURES

{FAT HEN}

It's not often that you compare the scenery of South West Cornwall to a supermarket. But under the tutelage of expert forager Caroline Davey you soon start to see the beaches, cliffs and moorland as a wild larder, and the best place to gather ingredients for a gourmet dinner. "I just want to show people the potential of wild ingredients in the kitchen. It's about using foraged foods like any other ingredients you would buy from the supermarket, and making interesting, delicious dishes with them," says Caroline.

A keen cook with a background in ecology and botany, Caroline conceived Fat Hen in 2007, originally supplying local restaurants with her foraged ingredients. "I got – and still get – a lot of inspiration from working with talented and creative chefs using wild ingredients," she says. By 2008 she was running her own foraging and wild cookery courses, and now her repertoire has expanded to include all sorts of disciplines from seaweed, shellfish and game, to wild Italian cookery. The name Fat Hen comes from the name of a wild edible green that was one of Britain's staple crops about 2,000 years ago, and it still flourishes here in Cornwall after the potato crop.

Caroline's renovated barns in St Buryan are the perfect base for the courses; her huge country kitchen sitting right on the doorstep of West Cornwall's prime foraging territory. "As well as gathering ingredients along the shoreline in places like Marazion, we also run foraging trips on bikes from here – usually cycling about 20 miles on a loop via Sennen, where we top up our ingredients with a fresh crab or fish from the fishermen there," Caroline explains.

On a typical foraging day you might spend the morning gathering greens, herbs, salad, veg, seaweeds, flowers, seeds and roots, before returning to cook them up into restaurant-worthy dishes. "I love helping people appreciate the ingredients that are out there. People start identifying edible plants in a bunch of greenery or seaweed and realise not only that they can eat them, but that they actually taste really good," says Caroline. "More people want to forage these days. It's the natural progression from the organic movement. People have more desire to know where their food has come from," she says.

"THE PROFILE OF WILD FOOD IS CHANGING. IT'S REALLY EXCITING TO SEE MORE CHEFS USING IT, WHICH MAKES IT MORE VALID."

As more people open their eyes to our edible landscape, it's not just eating wild food that's important; it's the process of foraging for our own ingredients that is changing, and emphasising, our relationship with food and our environment. "I love being outside foraging," says Caroline. "Being out and having a connection with the landscape and food feels so good – and so right. When you get down to the beach and you're out foraging you're living so much in the moment, everything feels perfect."

Rabbit Loin with a Mustard and Cream Sauce, Wild Spinach & Nettle Gnocchi

This is a great wild food recipe and isn't season dependent, as there's no closed season for hunting rabbits. As rabbits are shot for pest control it's a plentiful meat and never in short supply. This recipe uses the leanest part of the rabbit (the loin) which is rather like the breast of a chicken and needs very little cooking.

I love to combine the local greens – nettles and wild spinach – with wild rabbit shot just a few fields away. Everything is as fresh as can be and all the ingredients have come from within a few miles or metres of my kitchen.

(Serves 4)

Ingredients

- 4 rabbits skinned and jointed, loins removed.
- 50g (1.8oz) butter
- 2 cloves of garlic finely chopped
- 1 tblsp flat leaved parsley, finely chopped
- 1 tbsp thyme, finely chopped
- 1 tsp whole grain mustard
- Splash of white wine
- 3 tbsps double cream
- Large bunch of wild spinach (sea beet)
- Just over 1kg (2.3lbs) potatoes (choose a floury variety such as King Edward or Maris piper).
- 300g (10.5oz) plain flour
- 2 egg yolks
- A bunch of nettles
- 50g (1.9oz) parmesan
- Salt and pepper

Method

Gnocchi:

1. Wash and blanch the nettles in salted boiling water for 1 minute. Drain, squeeze out as much excess water as you can from the nettles and chop them finely.
2. Boil the potatoes in their skins – until just cooked erring on the side of undercooked. Peel the skins and pass the potatoes through a potato ricer. Put the potato into a large bowl.
3. Add the flour, egg yolks, chopped nettles, grated parmesan and salt.
4. Bring together all the ingredients with your hands to form a dough. Turn the dough out onto a floured worktop and knead it bringing in plain flour to stop it sticking.
5. Break off small balls of dough and roll out into a long sausage shape on the worktop. Cut pieces off the 'sausage' all the way along.
6. Roll each piece up the back of a fork using the back of a teaspoon. Roll it the alternate way to the knife cut to get the lines across the gnocchi.
7. Blanch in boiling salted water. The gnocchi are ready when they float to the top of the pan.
8. Either serve now, or if you want to use them later or pan fry them (which is totally delicious and the way I like them), put them straight into a bowl of cold water to stop them continuing to cook, drain and run through a further jug of cold water. Set aside.

   If you want to store them drain off the water and mix the gnocchi with some olive oil. You can store them like this overnight in an airtight container in the fridge.

   When you want to serve the gnocchi heat some butter and olive oil in a frying pan on a medium heat. Add the gnocchi and sear each piece until golden, turning once during cooking.

Rabbit:

1. Remove the loins from the saddle of a rabbit and set aside the other parts of the rabbit to be used in other recipes.
2. Heat the butter in a frying pan until melted and quite hot. Add the garlic, parsley and thyme and cook gently for a minute. Then add the rabbit loins and cook for a couple of minutes on each side, remove to a warm plate.
3. Pour the white wine into the frying pan. Stir and reduce. Add the cream and the mustard, stir and reduce.
4. Season to taste. Put the rabbit loins back into the pan, stir and cover with the sauce.

Wild spinach:

1. Whilst you are preparing the sauce put a large pan of salted water on to boil for the wild spinach.
2. When the water has boiled add the spinach for 2 minutes, drain, put back into the pan and add a splash of olive oil, a squeeze of lemon juice, salt and pepper.

To serve:

Serve the rabbit on top of a bed of wild spinach with the gnocchi surrounding it.

Laver Seaweed and Pancetta Cakes with Wild Garlic or Fennel & Mussel Sauce

Laver seaweed has to be up there with my top 3 seaweeds and it features heavily on most of my menus. It's very versatile and can be roasted, fried and boiled. You can 'go Welsh' and boil it or 'go far eastern' and roast, fry or air dry it. It's very closely related to Japanese nori so this is our 'Cornish nori.' It has a deeply savoury, mineral rich flavor. This recipe is my take on the Welsh laver bread. I simmer the seaweed for a couple of hours to tenderize it but I don't boil it all day like they do in Wales as I prefer the texture of the seaweed to come through. This recipe is for a lunch starter but it can equally be served for breakfast without the sauce but with a poached egg on top.

Serves 4 as a starter

- Small bowl of cooked laver seaweed (enough to form into 4 fishcake-sized patties)
- 1 small onion
- Scattering of oatmeal
- 2 pieces of pancetta or smoked bacon
- Squeeze of lemon juice
- 1 egg
- White breadcrumbs
- Oil for frying
- Knob of butter
- Salt & pepper
- 16 mussels
- 150ml (¼pt) good quality dry cider
- 300ml (¼pt) double cream
- 1 tsp Dijon mustard
- 1 tbsp chopped wild garlic or wild fennel fronds

1. Pick laver seaweed from the rocks. Take home and wash very well. This may need up to 8 washes to remove all the sand and small creatures hiding amongst the fronds.
2. Once washed put the laver into a saucepan and simmer on a gentle heat for 2 hours until tender but still with some texture. You may not need to add any water to the seaweed as it will hold quite a lot of water naturally. However, check to ensure it doesn't stick to the pan. If it does stick add some water.
3. Whilst the laver is cooking trim and chop some smoked bacon, fry until crispy, set aside.
4. Saute the onion until caramelised.
5. Add the bacon, onion, oatmeal, butter, salt and pepper & lemon juice to the warm laver seaweed and stir until thoroughly mixed and the butter has melted.
6. Cool and leave in the fridge for at least an hour or overnight.
7. Remove from the fridge and make the mixture into fishcake sized patties. Dip into whisked egg followed by breadcrumbs and lay on a try until ready to fry.
8. Fry the laver cakes until golden, place in a warm oven to keep hot.
9. Now make the sauce. Get a saucepan very hot on the stove. Throw in your cleaned mussels. Add the cider and cook until the mussels have opened. Remove the mussels and set aside.
10. Now reduce down the cider to half. Add the cream and mustard and reduce the cream by half. Season and add the chopped fennel fronds or wild garlic and the reserved mussels (out of their shells) at the end of cooking.
11. Serve the laver cake surrounded by a couple of spoons of the sauce.

Crab and Sea Lettuce Tagliatelle

I live three miles from Sennen Cove and during the summer there's nothing I like more than to pop down to the cove to pick up my crab from a local fisherman. I ring him the night before to place my order and he brings in crab, lobster and mackerel for me, fresh from the sea that morning. I love to go direct to the source for all my ingredients. The other wild ingredients in this dish are sea lettuce (seaweed), rock samphire and wild fennel. These three ingredients are all coastal and have a real affinity for seafood. It makes perfect sense to me to serve ingredients growing on the seashore with crab freshly brought in from the sea a few metres away.

Serves 4

Ingredients

For this recipe you also require a pasta machine

- Meat from 1 large brown crab or 2 large spider crabs (both white and brown) or 120g (4oz) picked white crab meat, 50g (1.8oz) brown meat
- 1 red chilli, deseeded and finely chopped
- 2 cloves garlic, finely chopped
- Juice of 1 lemon
- 100ml Olive oil
- 300ml light chicken stock
- Handful of wild fennel fronds, chopped
- Handful of rock samphire, chopped
- 150g (5oz) sea lettuce
- Salt and pepper
- 400g (14oz) '00' pasta flour
- ½ tsp salt
- 3-4 whole eggs
- 1 tsp olive oil

Method

1. Boil 100g of the sea lettuce until tender (15 minutes). Liquidise the sea lettuce with a little water. Pass the green liquid through a muslin cloth and retain the green puree left in the cloth.
2. Mix the sea lettuce puree, flour, salt, eggs & olive oil in a bowl and bring together to form a dough.
3. Turn the dough onto a table and knead until it is smooth and shiny (10–15 minutes). Cover in cling film and leave to rest in the fridge for at least one hour (no more than 24 hours). Pasta dough freezes really well so if you have any excess you can freeze it at this point.
4. Roll the dough through a pasta machine starting on the widest setting. Roll it through this setting about 5 times, each time folding the dough back on itself before feeding it into the machine.
5. Now run the dough through each of the settings until you get to the penultimate setting.
6. Now run each sheet of pasta through the taglietelle cutter. Once cut drape the tagliatelle over the back of a chair or broom to air dry for a few minutes to prevent it sticking together and clumping up.
7. If you are preparing the crab yourself, bring a large pan of heavily salted water (10g per litre to mimic the salinity of sea water) to the boil.
8. Dispatch your live crab by skewering through the depression behind the tail and also between the eyes.
9. Place the crab in the boiling water and cook for approximately 15 minutes once the water comes to the boil again.
10. Remove the cooked crab, leave to cool and pick out the meat.
11. Pick through the crabmeat to make sure it's free from any bits of shell
12. Bring a large pan of salted water to the boil ready for the tagliatelle.
13. In a sauté pan heat the olive oil. Add the chilli and garlic and cook until softened without browning, stirring regularly. Add the remaining sea lettuce (chopped), rock samphire and fennel fronds and cook gently for a minute or so. Then add the brown crab meat. Add the chicken stock and lemon juice to the pan and bring to the boil.
14. Meanwhile cook the fresh pasta in the boiling salted water for 3 minutes. Once cooked drain and add to the pan with the other ingredients including the white crab meat. Toss together until everything is evenly mixed. Taste and season. Loosen with a little of the cooking water if the pasta looks too dry.

Carragheen Panna Cotta with Blackberry Compote

I always marvel at the properties of carragheen seaweed and its ability to thicken and set other ingredients. Most of you will have eaten carragheen inadvertently as it's a food additive used in many processed ice-creams and desserts. I love to use carragheen for panna cotta as it creates a lovely soft set (if you don't use too much) and it negates the need for gelatine, which is fantastic if you're cooking for vegetarians.

Blackberries, in my opinion, are one of the finest wild foods and I've had a love affair with them since my childhood. I still don't think you can beat blackberry jam on thick doorsteps of white toast dripping with butter! It was a bumper blackberry year this year and my freezer is full of them. They go so well with this panna cotta. The sweet geranium imparts a delicate floral background note to the blackberries.

Serves 6

Ingredients

Panna cotta

- 6 moulds – these can be ramekins, coffee cups, small bowls or darioles
- Handful of dried carragheen seaweed
- 300ml (½pt) double cream
- 300ml (½pt) whole milk
- 50g (2oz) caster sugar
- 1 vanilla pod
- 1 strip of lemon peel - no pith

Blackberry compote

- 100g (3½oz) sugar
- 100ml (3½fl oz) water
- 150g (5oz) blackberries
- 2 sweet geranium leaves

Method

Panna Cotta

1. Soak the carragheen in warm water until soft and slightly jelly-like.
2. Warm the milk and cream gently with the sugar, lemon peel and vanilla to dissolve and infuse respectively.
3. Drain the carragheen well and add to the milk and cream - gently bring to the boil. Simmer gently for 10 minutes and when the mixture begins to thicken (it should coat the back of a spoon or the side of the pan), remove from the heat and strain into a jug.
4. Immediately pour the mixture into moulds.
5. Allow to cool and thicken. These can be refrigerated for later on if required.
6. To turn out the panna cotta you may need to dip the mould into hot water to loosen and press gently around the outside edge of the panna cotta to release from the side of the mould. Turn out onto a plate.

Blackberry Compote

1. Add the sugar to the water in a saucepan and heat until the sugar has dissolved into a sugar syrup.
2. Wash and pick over the blackberries, discarding any hard, unripe or mushy berries.
3. Add the blackberries to the sugar syrup with the sweet geranium leaves and poach gently for 20 minutes.
4. Leave to cool and serve with the panna cotta.

WE ❤ CORNISH CRABS

The Fat Hen's Caroline Davey gets her fresh crabs from the fishermen at Sennen and Newlyn. Based on Newlyn's quayside, Harvey & Sons has been sourcing the best shellfish from fishermen all over the county for 60 years, and supplies crabs to restaurants all around Cornwall and the rest of the UK.

"CATCHING CRABS IS ENVIRONMENTALLY SOUND, PASSIVE FISHING – THERE IS NO BY-CATCH AND ANYTHING THAT IS TOO SMALL GETS PUT BACK INTO THE SEA TO CARRY ON BREEDING," explains Paul Harvey, one of the trio of brothers that run this family business. Many of his customers favour the white meat, but the brown crab meat is better for soups and crab cakes, while the waxy, red meat from the hen crabs tends to be sweeter and is full of iron too.

John Tonkin, a crab fisherman from Cadgwith, supplies much of his catch to Harvey & Sons. Crabbing off the Lizard for as many days of the year as the weather and tides permit, he can haul in around 400 crabs a day. "I've been crabbing for about 24 years and it's a good living," says John. "In summer, when you're out on the ocean as the sun comes up, there's nowhere better to be on the whole planet. Sometimes we get dolphins and porpoises around the boat – we've even seen a fin whale and its baby."

Not only does John get a buzz from hauling in shellfish, he's also keen to emphasise that it's a very sustainable way of fishing: "We only take what is good and the rest goes back alive," he says. "It's nonsense that we're running out of fish – there's more fish now than there was when I started. We've just had our best crab season in years. Nature is very good at looking after itself."

James Bosustow – one of Newlyn's fishermen who supplies Harvey & Sons as well as selling his catch in the market – agrees that there is no shortage of fish off the coast of Cornwall: "There's masses of fish out there lately," says James. "Hake and haddock are coming back in abundance, and just off Newlyn we get plenty of monkfish, turbot, brill, pollock and ling."

CAROLINE'S TIPS ON HOW TO PREPARE YOUR CRABS

- **Put the crab in the freezer for about one hour.** This makes the crab sleepy and is the most humane way of preparing it.
- **To minimise the suffering of the crab, I prefer to kill it immediately before cooking.** To do this, in quick succession, insert a skewer and wiggle it, firstly into the depression below the tail and then between the eyes.
- **Once it stops moving, put the crab straight into a large pan of salted water on a rolling boil.** Bring the water back to the boil and cook for 20 minutes.
- **Remove the crab and leave to cool.**
- **Twist and break off the claws and legs from the body.** Put the body to one side.
- **The claw is in three sections.** Break off the section closest to the body, put to one side and place the remainder of the claw on a chopping board. Give the claw a sharp tap with a rolling pin/small hammer to crack the shell.
- **Pull the two remaining sections apart and, using a crab pick or the handle of a teaspoon, ease the meat away from the shell into a bowl.** Repeat for the first section. Be careful not to break the thin cartilage of the claw into the crabmeat.
- **Follow a similar pattern for the legs.**
- **Prize the crab shell away from the body, drain any water from the shell and scoop the brown meat into a bowl.** Using a fork, mix the brown meat into a paste.
- **Remove grey gills (or dead man's fingers) from the body and discard.** Despite the name these are not actually poisonous, merely tough and indigestible. Carefully tease the white meat from the leg cavities and body comb.
- **Chill the crabmeat before eating.**

Top tip: A clean pair of mole grips is useful for cracking claws and legs too. You can adjust the pressure to ensure the shell cracks but does not shatter, making it less likely that you will end up with shell in your crabmeat.

A WINE FOR ALL SEASONS

TRY THESE SEASONAL WINES TO SUIT THE CHANGING WEATHER

Fabulous seasonal food deserves to be paired with wonderful wine. Jon Keast of Scarlet Wines talks us through perfect wines for every season.

SPRING
Hunter Valley Semillon
In the Hunter Valley they pick the Semillon very young so it tastes incredibly fresh. These light wines with intense lemon and lime flavours go perfectly with shellfish.
Jon recommends: Tyrells Brookdale Semillon, Hunter Valley, Australia

Mencia
Harking from northwest Spain, this is a quaffable, good value wine made from fresh, tangy raspberry fruit. It pairs well with seafood and salads.
Jon recommends: Castro Ventosa Mencia Joven, Bierzo, Spain

SUMMER
Cava
Camel Valley's award-winning Brut gets a lot of attention as Cornwall's very own bubbly and makes a fantastic, clean summer drink. But get your hands on a quality Cava from a small producer, and enjoy cutting freshness alongside rich flavours and an earthier taste. Perfect with fish and chips.
Jon recommends: Babot Brut Nature Cava, Penedés, Spain

Rosé
Crisp, delicate and fruity with a salmon-pink colouring, a Provence Rosé complements lots of light, summer dishes.
Jon recommends: Chateau Beaulieu Rose, Provence, France

Sherry and ice cream
A luscious, sweet sherry, full of caramel and raisin flavours, can be poured over ice cream as a delicious summer dessert.
Jon recommends: Valdespino, El Candado Pedro Ximinex, Jerez, Spain

AUTUMN
Chianti

Chianti Classico is a Sangiovese-based wine with hints of tobacco, spice flavours and plummy fruit. Ideal for autumn dining it goes well with roasts and game.
Jon recommends: Castellare, Chianti Classico, Tuscany, Italy

Tokaji Furmint

This fresh, dry white has lots of honey and a nutty complexity too. It goes well with mushrooms and crostini.
Jon recommends: Dobogo Furmint, Tokaji, Hungary

WINTER
Tawny Port

A 10 year-old tawny port is an elegant mellow drink with flavours of cooked fruit and spices. Delicious with cheese or to sip by a roaring log fire.
Jon recommends: Churchill's 10 Year Old Tawny, Douro, Portugal

Lirac Rhone

Gentle and enjoyable, with rich fruit, nice length and a little spice from the Syrah, this makes a wonderful winter wine.
Jon recommends: Famille Brechet, Moulin des Chenes Lirac, Rhone, France

SEEK, GATHER & EXPLORE!

Forage for edible treasures amongst the hedgerows and beaches. Here are Caroline's favourite ingredients:

ELDERFLOWER

The taste and scent of English summer. The sweet flavour of elderflower makes delicious cordial and non-alcoholic elderflower 'champagne', and can also be used in salads and dressings.

TREE MALLOW

The coast is strewn with tree mallows; you'll find them in every beach car park you visit. The tall knobby trunk looks prehistoric and both the leaves and flowers are edible. The flowers have a gorgeous purple hue and add great colour to a summer salad.

APPLE MINT

A versatile ingredient for cocktails and summer barbecues. Apple mint adds zingy flavour to salad dishes, cocktails and meat; or simply pour boiling water over a sprig for fresh mint tea.

BLACK MUSTARD

Strong and peppery. Use the flowers in a salad or a Bloody Mary, and use the leaves for frittatas, salads or as a cooked green.

ROCK SAMPHIRE

Named after St Pierre (the patron saint of fishermen), samphire
is delicious pickled, in a salsa verde, in fritters or alongside
fresh fish.

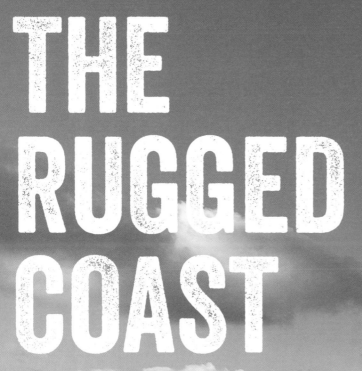

THE RUGGED COAST

QUOITS, WITCHES, MERMAIDS AND HEARTY FOOD IN STAUNCH STONE SNUGS

GOURMET PUB GRUB ON CORNWALL'S WILDEST COASTLINE

West Penwith is home to some of the most remote, rugged and beguiling landscapes in the county. While visitors trickle along the south coast bound for Land's End, its north shore between Sennen and St Ives remains wild and desolate: The coast path climbs and falls past the eerie remains of Cornwall's mining industry, jagged cliffs jut into the full force of the Atlantic, and quoit-smattered moorland tumbles to coves steeped in legends of mermaids and smugglers.

This is a landscape that beckons adventurous souls: Rock climbers scale the spine of Commando Ridge at Bosigran and walkers don sturdy boots to explore calf-busting terrain and clap eyes on seals and seabirds. It's a place of artists and eccentrics too – DH Lawrence fell in love with the rustic village of Zennor and painters commit the rich coastal scenes to canvas. THE PEOPLE WHO RESIDE HERE ARE A HARDY BREED, REARING CATTLE AND COAXING AN ABUNDANCE OF CROPS FROM THE LAND. This is a place where the food is as wild and natural as the landscape – fields are ablaze with greens and edible flowers, while hedgerows are bursting with berries and herbs. Restaurants of St Ives and Penzance only have to cast their nets a few miles west to gather some of the finest ingredients in the country.

COMFORT FOOD

{THE GURNARD'S HEAD}

Wrapped in the wild and mystical landscape of West Penwith, The Gurnard's Head has good reason to lure foodies beyond the trappings of St Ives and Penzance.

This rustic inn, painted beacon yellow, sits on a winding country lane just off the coast path. The ocean crashes in the distance. Cows graze outside the window. "A place like this needs to be a proper watering hole," says Charles Inkin, one of the brothers behind the EATDRINKSLEEP enterprise, which includes The Old Coastguard in nearby Mousehole, as well as The Gurnard's Head. "People need to walk in and feel warm and welcome. They need a big bowl of stew, a pint of well-looked after beer, a log fire and somewhere to dry their walking boots." And that's exactly what he's created - a welly walks and log fire kind of pub, with fine Cornish food at its heart.

Head chef, Matthew Smith, has quite a simple approach to cooking: "We're not fine dining; we're just very good quality. We're the sort of place you can come in with your dog and muddy wellies, and

have a hearty soup or a decent terrine," he says. "I let the ingredients do the talking.

WHEN YOU'RE USING THE BEST INGREDIENTS YOU DON'T HAVE TO DO MUCH TO THEM TO MAKE THEM TASTE GOOD. We favour simple food like local sausages with beetroot, mash potato and a homemade sauce."

There's an intimate link between the landscape and the menu, bridged by a strong relationship with the local fishermen and farmers. Some of the veg comes from the community-run Bosavern Farm in St Just, and seafood is sourced from the local day boats where possible. "This place ticks through re-investing in the community and keeping the economy local," says Charles.

Cooking with the seasons and plucking ingredients from the surroundings is simply common sense in this location. "The availability and quality of ingredients down here is incredible," says Matt, as he cooks up mackerel that was line-caught that morning on a feather in Sennen Cove. "The suppliers not only care about their produce but they are so knowledgeable too. It rivals anywhere in the country." Building his menus around what's available locally, he also uses plenty of foraged ingredients, including mushrooms, sea beet, samphire and three-

cornered leeks. "Upwards of 60% of our ingredients come from this western toe of Cornwall," he says.

Being a country pub, the beer and wine is important too. A cracking wine list includes wines from less-explored regions available by the carafe, and the beer is well sourced and well kept. "We stock Skinners because it's local and we love it," says Charles, "and we're one of very few places that stock the local Skreach cider made down the road in St. Buryan. There are also ales from Penryn's Rebel Brewing Company, and the Cornish-made Tarquin's Gin and Pastis behind the bar.

"Look where we are – it's a magical place at the very end of Cornwall," says Charles. "You can see why artists and poets are drawn here – people who want to get lost and live a bohemian existence." But, as The Gurnard's Head proves, this isn't just a place to dip a toe in Cornwall's wildest, most alluring landscape; it's also a place where you can slip into a very civilised inn and enjoy fantastic food that comes from the scenery around you.

Line Caught Sennen Mackerel, Pickled Vegetables, and Lemon Crème Fraîche

From shore to the door, this mackerel was caught less than three miles away.

Ingredients

- Pickled Vegetables:
- 1 Carrot
- 1 kohlrabi (part of the cabbage family)
- 1 banana shallot
- 500ml (18fl oz) white wine
- 500ml (18fl oz) white wine vinegar
- 500g (2oz) caster sugar
- 1 bay leaf
- 2 allspice berries
- 1 star anise

Crème fraîche:

- 200g (7oz) crème fraîche
- 200g (7oz) double cream
- ½ lemon
- Salt and pepper

Method

1. For the pickling solution place the white wine, white wine vinegar and sugar in a small saucepan. Add the bay leaf, allspice and star anise and heat until sugar has dissolved.
2. Remove from the heat and cover with clingfilm. This will allow the flavours to infuse.
3. Peel and slice the vegetables thinly. Wash the shallot under cold water (which will remove some of the strong onion flavour).
4. While the pickling solution is still warm add the vegetables.
5. Stored in an airtight container in the fridge, the vegetables will keep for a week.

Crème fraîche:

Add the cream to the crème fraîche. Whisk until there are stiff peaks and season with the lemon juice and salt and pepper.

Mackerel:

Source some good quality mackerel fillets from a local fish supplier – the fresher the better. Ask the fishmonger to fillet and V bone the fish.

1. To cook the mackerel simply turn your grill to full and season the fillets with salt and pepper. Lightly oil and place on a baking tray. Grill the mackerel for 1 minute on each side – a little longer if the fillets are big. Don't be scared if the skin blisters and starts to blacken. This is the desired effect and tastes great.
2. Immediately remove from the grill, dress with the pickled vegetables and serve with a dollop of crème fraîche.

Line Caught Sea Bass, Gnocchi, Shoreline Vegetables, Bouillabaisse & Chorizo Aioli

Seabass is such a versatile fish. It's more than capable of handling pairing with strong flavour. This particular fish was line caught from a day boat in St Ives Bay, a method that's not only sustainable but also ensures the fish reaches us in the best possible quality.

Chorizo Aioli Ingredients

- 200g (7oz) good quality chorizo
- 2tsp Dijon mustard
- 2 cloves garlic, grated
- ½ tsp salt
- 3 tbsp white wine vinegar
- 2 tbsp lemon juice
- 3 egg yolks
- 350ml (12floz) sunflower oil
- 50ml (2floz) olive oil
- 20ml (1floz) warm water
- 1 pinch smoked paprika

Method

1. In the restaurant we always make the aioli using a food processor, but it works just as well by hand.
2. Chop the chorizo into small cubes and place in a small saucepan, then add the olive oil and 150ml of the cooking oil.
3. Leave on low heat for about 20 minutes to allow the colour and flavour to bleed from the chorizo into the oil. Don't get it too hot or it will burn the chorizo and the flavour will become bitter. Leave to cool.
4. Place the eggs, white wine vinegar, mustard, garlic and lemon juice in a mixing bowl or food processor.
5. Whisk/blend till combined and pale. Slowly add the other 200ml of cooking oil. If at any point it begins to look really thick, use a little of the warm water to let it down.
6. Pass the oil off the chorizo and then gently add that as well, make sure the oil is no warmer than room temperature. Finish by folding in the diced chorizo.
7. This will keep in the fridge in an airtight tub/jar for around a week. Also goes great with cold meats. I love it on chicken sandwiches.

Bouillabaisse Sauce Ingredients

- 1 large onion, chopped
- 2 carrots, chopped
- 1 bulb of fennel, chopped
- 2 sticks of celery, chopped
- ½ leek, chopped
- 3 cloves garlic, chopped in half
- 3 tbsp tomato puree
- ½ bottle white wine
- 100ml (3½floz) Pernod
- 1 star anise
- ½ tbsp coriander seeds
- ½ tsp cayenne pepper
- Pinch saffron
- 1 orange
- 20g (½oz) fresh tarragon
- 1.5ltr (2.6pt) fish stock
- 700g (1lb 9oz) tinned tomatoes

Method

1. Take the vegetables and sweat in a large pan, add the spices and leave for 2 minutes. Add the tomato puree and booze and reduce by half. Add the stock and tinned tomatoes and simmer for 30 minutes or until the vegetables are tender.
2. Blend in a food processor and pass through a fine sieve. Season, then finish with a squeeze of fresh orange juice and chopped tarragon.

Gnocchi Ingredients

- 300g (11oz) mash potato
- 90g (3oz) 'OO' pasta flour
- 60g (2oz) grated Parmesan
- ½ egg
- ½ egg yolk
- 1tsp salt
- 10g (½oz) chopped tarragon

Method

1. Gnocchi works best when the mash potato is hot, so

the secret is to get all the other ingredients weighed out first and mix them together in one big bowl.

2. When the mash is ready combine it with the rest of the ingredients and knead it into a ball.

3. Lightly flour the surface and roll out into sausage shapes. Using a knife cut into sections.

4. Drop them into salted, boiling water and when they float, they are done. Remove with a spoon.

5. They can be eaten like this, however, in this recipe we gently pan fry them to give them a crisp outside.

SEA BASS:

1. Good fresh sea bass should have bright red gills, shiny clear eyes and be firm to touch. Ask your fishmonger to scale, fillet and debone the fish.

2. Season the sea bass with salt and place in a hot non-stick pan skin side down. Leave for 3 minutes, and then place in a pre-warmed hot oven (180C) for roughly 4 minutes. This is based on a 150g piece of Sea bass. Obviously a bigger or particularly thick piece would take longer.

To serve:

Place a ladle of the bouillabaisse sauce on the bottom of the bowl/plate. Scatter with gnocchi and some lightly blanched shoreline vegetables – I like to use samphire and three-cornered leek. Place the sea bass on top and then a dollop of the aioli.

Malt Chocolate Cheesecake, Honeycomb, Raspberries, and Yoghurt Sorbet

Velvety smooth, rich chocolate cheesecake paired with sweet Cornish raspberries. A great way to round off any meal.

Cheesecake:
Base:
- 150g (5oz) Hobnobs, smashed
- 25g (1oz) caster sugar
- 50g (2oz) unsalted Butter

Cake:
- 125g (4½oz) cream cheese
- 1 egg yolk
- 25g (1oz) caster sugar
- 190ml (6½fl oz) double cream, semi-whipped
- 125g (4½oz) 70% dark chocolate, melted

1. Melt the sugar and butter on a gentle heat then combine with the smashed Hobnobs. Set in a clingfilm-lined tray.
2. For the cheesecake, whisk the eggs and sugar until pale and fluffy. Fold in the cream cheese, and then fold in the melted dark chocolate. When all are combined fold in the double cream.
3. Pour into the pre-lined tray and bake in a water lined tray 'Bain Marie' for 20 minutes at 100C.
4. Chill before cutting.

Honeycomb:
- 160g (5½oz) caster sugar
- 25g (1oz) honey
- 60g (2oz) glucose
- 30ml (1fl oz) water
- ½ tsp bicarbonate of soda

1. Before you start making honeycomb, it's always an idea to get everything ready. Line a good sized baking tray with high sides (or a silicone baking mould) with greaseproof paper. Remember when you add the bicarbonate of soda it will increase the mix to roughly quadruple its size.
2. Place all ingredients except the bicarbonate of soda in a pan. Place on a low heat, until all the sugar is dissolved. Then increase the temperature and, using a sugar thermometer, take the solution to 148C.
3. Add the bicarbonate of soda, and using a whisk stir the pan 3 times and then pour out into the mould/tin.
4. Place in a cool location for at least 30 minutes to allow setting. Then turn out and break up as required.

Yoghurt Sorbet
- 250g natural yoghurt
- 15g (½oz) double cream
- 12g (½oz) icing sugar
- 15g (½oz) milk

Place the milk, cream and icing sugar in a pan and heat till the sugar has dissolved. Fold in the yogurt and churn in an ice-cream machine.

To serve:
Place a piece of cheesecake on a plate and garnish with fresh raspberries, the broken honeycomb and a scoop of yogurt sorbet.

Soda Bread

Charles brought this recipe back from Ireland after spending time with celebrated Irish chef and author Darina Allen at Ballymaloe in County Cork. Give it a go – it's the simplest bread to make.

This will make about 5 small loaves

Ingredients

- 325g (11½oz) rye flour
- 325g (11½oz) stoneground wholemeal flour
- 750g (26½oz) plain flour
- 20g (½oz) salt
- 30g (1oz) bicarbonate of soda
- 1L (1¾pt) buttermilk
- 50ml (2fl oz) luke warm water

Method

1. Place all dry ingredients in a bowl. Mix well. Make a well in the middle of the mix and pour in the buttermilk and water. Stir to combine and then turn out onto a floured surface. Divide into 5 without kneading and place on a baking tray. Bake at 180C for 15 minutes. Turn and give a further 15 minutes.
2. Cool on a wire rack.

CAULIFLOWER
TURNIP
THE BEET

Support local farmers

TIPS: FARM-TO-FORK FOOD

Both The Gurnard's Head and The Old Coastguard source much of their produce from the farms of West Penwith – beef from Pendeen, pork from The Primrose Herd in Busveal, free-range chickens from Morvah and fresh produce from local growers including Bosavern Community Farm.

Head chef Matthew Smith recommends speaking to your local butchers and fishmongers to find out about meats that are sourced locally, and different ways to use different types, and cuts, of meat and fish. "For example, as you come into autumn and winter you get a lot more wide, round fish, such as cod and pollock, so that's what you should be looking for if you want something landed locally. Then in spring and summer you get more mackerel and flat fish," Matt explains.

When it comes down to cooking farm-to-fork ingredients, Matt suggests keeping it simple and letting the flavours speak for themselves. "There's no need to overcomplicate things – if you've got a good ingredient you don't have to do a lot to it," he says.

COCKTAIL HOUR

{TARQUIN'S GIN & PASTIS}

Glance behind the bar at The Gurnard's Head, and you'll find that they spend as much time meticulously sourcing the best local drinks as they do gathering ingredients for their kitchen. And it's not just local ales and ciders – Tarquin's handcrafted Cornish Gin and Pastis are two local spirits making a hit on the drinks list.

Handmade in small batches on the north coast of Cornwall, these contemporary spirits are named after the founder and head distiller at the Southwestern Distillery – Tarquin himself. Using the traditional techniques of a copper still pot fired by flame, the result is complex, aromatic spirits that have been lovingly crafted.

The gin is distilled with handpicked Devon violets and fresh orange zest, and diluted to bottling strength with pure Cornish spring water. "We use lots of citrus fruits – fresh grapefruit, lemons, orange zest and homegrown violets – as well as other aromatics like the juniper, which gives our gin its characteristic flavour," explains Athene Lippiett, Tarquin's sister and business partner. A modern take on the French anise classic, the Cornish Pastis is the UK's first ever pastis, made using foraged gorseflowers from the cliff tops, orange zest and a touch of liquorice root. Enjoy it with ice and water, or try one of Tarquin's more adventurous cocktails.

Tarquin's Cocktail O'clock

NEGRONI

A complex drink with bitter and sweet notes, herbs and spices – and additional citrus notes from Tarquin's Gin.

• 1 part Tarquin's Gin
• 1 part sweet vermouth
• 1 part bitters (Campari)

Mix equal measures of the spirits over ice. Serve with an orange slice.

CORNISH 75

This uplifting and refreshing cocktail is traditionally known as a French 75. To make it more Cornish a local sparkling wine could be used.

• 30ml Tarquin's Gin
• 2 dashes sugar syrup
• 15ml lemon juice
• 60ml Prosecco

Combine gin, syrup, and lemon juice in a cocktail shaker filled with ice. Shake vigorously and strain into an iced champagne glass. Top up with Prosecco. Stir gently. Garnish with a lemon twist.

THE CORNISH PASTICHE

Created by David Smith from Hix Fish House in Lyme Regis, this is delicious anytime as an apéritif or with seafood.

• 2 shots Cornish Pastis
• 150ml apple juice
• 1 lime, squeezed for juice
• Lots of fresh mint

Muddle together and serve in a long glass over ice.

THE TARQUINI

This recipe combines Tarquin's Gin and Pastis in one delicious cocktail that balances floral and aromatic flavours.

• 2 shots Tarquin's Gin
• 3 dashes Cornish Pastis
• 15ml dry vermouth
• 3 dashes Crème de Violette

Stir over ice. Strain into a coupe glass. Garnish with a lemon twist.

DOG FRIENDLY DINING

Welcoming welly-clad walkers with hounds in tow, The Gurnard's Head is surrounded by some of the county's finest walking territory. Make it a pit-stop on a coast path tramp, or strike out from here on a stunning two-pub loop where you can march out to the headland and follow two miles of jaw-dropping coastline to Zennor, enjoy a pint at The Tinners Arms (www.tinnersarms.com), then take a short cut back across the fields and moorland.

Here are five of our favourite paw-friendly pubs with great walks on the doorstep:

■ THE TRAVELLERS REST, TREVARRIAN

Nestled between Mawgan Porth and Watergate Bay, this 18th century pub has always got St Austell ales and a stash of dog treats behind the bar. Head seaward along the footpath between its village location and Beacon Cove, and you'll be rewarded with eye-popping coastal scenery from Newquay Bay to Trevose Head. Turn west to Watergate Bay or east to Mawgan Porth – either way your efforts will earn you a pint and a portion of delicious Cornish pub grub when you loop back to The Travellers.
www.travellersrestcornwall.com

■ THE BUSH INN, MORWENSTOW

The 7.5-miles from Bude to Morwenstow is a strenuous undertaking on foot, tackling some gnarly sections of coast path. Tumbling waterfalls, the Hawker's Hut and a dramatic coastline littered with shipwrecks make every step worth the effort, especially when you veer inland at Morwenstow and stumble upon The Bush Inn – a dog-friendly 13th century pub serving CAMRA ales and hearty, homemade food.
www.thebushinnmorwenstow.com

■ THE DRIFTWOOD SPARS, ST AGNES

Hike over the cliffs from Perranporth to Trevaunance Cove, tracing old mining territory smattered with mine shafts and engine houses. Right on the coast path at the St Agnes end of the walk you'll find The Driftwood Spars – a traditional pub cum contemporary bistro, serving gourmet food, dog treats and ales from its own microbrewery.
www.driftwoodspars.com

■ RED RIVER INN, GWITHIAN

Surfers, walkers, families and dogs flock to this friendly village inn that sits behind three miles of pearly sands. A regular in the CAMRA Good Beer Guide, you can guarantee a decent pint from one of the Cornish microbreweries, as well as locally sourced pub grub and plenty of treats for the pooch, too.
www.red-river-inn.com

■ THE DEVONPORT INN, KINGSAND

Situated in a historic, traffic-free village, and yards from the beach, this cosy local pub peers out to the Rame Peninsula – stunning walking territory nudging the border between Cornwall and Devon. Classic, uncomplicated dishes, from ploughmans to Rame Head lobster, are served alongside well-kept local ales and a decent selection of wines.
www.devonportinn.com

USEFUL CONVERSION TABLES

Oven Temperature Conversions

Farenheit	Centigrade	Gas Mark	Description
225 F	110 C	¼	Very Cool
250 F	130 C	½	
275 F	140 C	1	Cool
300 F	150 C	2	
325 F	170 C	3	Very Moderate
350 F	180 C	4	Moderate
375 F	190 C	5	
400 F	200 C	6	Moderately Hot
425 F	220 C	7	Hot
450 F	230 C	8	
475 F	240 C	9	Very Hot

US Liquid Measurements

1 gallon	4 quarts	3.79 L (can round to 4L)
1 quart	2 pints	.95 L (can round to 1L)
1 pint	2 cups	16 fl. oz. or 450 ml
1 cup	8 fl oz	225 ml (can round to 250ml)
1 tablespoon (tbsp.)	½ fl oz	16 ml (can round to 15 ml)
1 teaspoon (tsp.)	⅓ tablespoon	5 ml

British Liquid Measurements

1 UK pint	0.56 ltrs	
1 UK liquid oz	0.96 US liquid oz	
1 pint	570 ml	16 fl oz
1 breakfast cup	10 fl oz	½ pint
1 tea cup	⅓ pint	
1 tablespoon	15 ml	
1 dessert spoon	10 ml	
1 teaspoon	5 ml	⅓ tablespoon
1 ounce	28.4 g	can round to 25 or 30
1 pound	454 g	
1 kg	2.2 pounds	

International Liquid Measurements

Country	Standard Cup	Standard Teaspoon	Standard Tablespoon
Canada	250 ml	5 ml	15 ml
Australia	250 ml	5 ml	20 ml
UK	250 ml	5 ml	15 ml
New Zealand	250 ml	5 ml	15 ml

USEFUL WEBSITES

7th Rise
Tregothnan
www.7thrise.co.uk

Fat Hen
St Buryan, 01736 810156
www.fathen.org

Good Vibes Café
Falmouth, 01326 211870
www.goodvibescafe.co.uk

Jam Jar
Newquay, 07580 907519
www.facebook.com/Jamjarnewquay

No.4
St Agnes, 01872 554245
www.no4peterville.co.uk

Origin Coffee
Helston
www.origincoffee.co.uk

Rebel Brewing Co
Penryn, 01326 378517
www.rebelbrewing.co.uk

Scott & Babs Wood Fired Food
Retorrick Mill, 01637 861598
www.facebook.com/scottandbabs

Seadrift
Porthleven, 01326 558733
www.seadriftporthleven.co.uk

Strong Adolfo's
Hawksfield, A39, 01208 816949
www.strongadolfos.com

Tarquin's Gin and Pastis
www.southwesterndistillery.com

The Beach Hut
Watergate, 01637 860877
www.watergatebay.co.uk

The Gurnard's Head
Nr Zennor, 01736 796928
www.gurnardshead.co.uk

INDEX

THANKS

Thanks to everyone who made this book happen; all the amazing chefs, food producers and entrepreneurs who gave up their time to inspire others to try great food and drink.

For us at Muse Media, working on this book has been a labour of love, so a big thanks to everyone involved: Hayley Spurway for making such beautiful Cornish food stories come to life; Mike Searle and his stunning photography; David Alcock for his impeccable design; Rhona and Excess Energy for spreading the word; cooking-whiz Sarah Hemsley for checking our recipes; and Jen Morgan, Meeche Hudd and Kelly Riddle for their tips on the classiest places to eat in Cornwall.

And most of all thanks to this magical county, Cornwall, for being such a fantastic place to have a foodie adventure!